SOLVAY

A GIANT

MAXIME RAPAILLE

S O L V A Y

A GIANT

Translated from French
by Romilly Harrisson

Collection Grands Formats

 DIDIER HATIER

This book was published under the original title of « *Solvay, un Géant* » by Didier Hatier publisher, Brussels 1989

© DIDIER HATIER, Bruxelles, 1990
  18, rue A. Labarre 1050 Bruxelles

D/1990/3030/29
ISBN 2-87088-701-9

I N T R O D U C T I O N

The extracted salt in brine solution arrives at the Group's oldest soda works in Couillet (Belgium), from Epe (West Germany). The Epe site is about sixty kilometers from the world's largest salt mine in Borth which is also a Solvay site. The other raw material, limestone, is found at the Couillet site where it is broken up, ground and sifted before being transferred to the lime kiln. The lime and carbon dioxide which are produced in these kilns are essential ingredients, together with salt brine and recycled ammonia, in the production of sodium carbonate. The solution is then dried and takes on its final aspect becoming a white powder, known as Solvay soda.

At the same time, on the other side of the world, man-made synthetics and drugs for medical purposes are produced by the Group's plants in a never-ending stream. Ultra-light bottles, futuristically-shaped gasoline storage tanks, vinyl wallpapers, leather goods, plastic pipes, clothing, vaccines, anti-depressants, anti-spasmodics, etc. are all coming off the production lines or are being developed in the Group's state-of-the-art laboratories. This enormous diversity would not surprise the man who was there at the start of it all and who was, during his own life-time, the prime mover.

The two aspects of his personality which give a good picture of Ernest Solvay are tenacity and very strong family ties. Add to these longevity, which was not a foregone conclusion, and we have the driving forces of his life which, even some 150 years later, is not yet over. Some people only leave memories, Ernest Solvay has left an enduring monument.

Perseverance is a natural quality in a man with a mission. What is more unusual is the fact that his father, mother, brothers and sisters not only gave him their moral encouragement but also their financial support.

What can one say of strangers — his investors — who after a moment's hesitation, yielded to his reasoning and gave him their wholehearted support? Without them, all would have come to nothing at one especially dramatic moment. We shall relate this incident in more detail later on. It is thanks to them that production started up again and that the initial failure at the Couillet site was soon a forgotten event. Their descendants and those of the original investors still represent over 50% of the company's shareholders — this is true today of only a very few companies.

It goes without saying that Ernest Solvay had enormous

10

powers of persuasion and also that he was no dreamer. By the time he was 20 years old, he was already an achiever — his motto was «Think to achieve». Those who believed in him, to the extent of entrusting him with their money, knew that he would go far in life, so far in fact that he would build an empire which 125 years on, is still as steady as a rock. What they saw before their deaths will have given them confidence in the company's stability. Even today, its expansion is extraordinary.

Ernest Solvay would have made a name as an artist or conqueror but few great painters, writers or composers enjoy fame during their own lifetimes and if they do, they are often forgotten for many years after their deaths. As for conquerors, history has given them a very bad reputation, calling them robbers (of land), murderers (of the indigenous people) and plunderers.

Ernest Solvay who was a scholar and scientist and only that, might very well have run the risk of being laughed at or rejected by historians, had history proved them right. He might have suffered the same fate as Leblanc who was his predecessor. Ernest Solvay possessed two other important qualities: he knew how to manage a company and he had total support from his remarkable family. His brother Alfred, above all, gave him his unmitigated assistance, dealing, right up to his death, with all the business matters and day-to-day management of the company, thus ensuring the stability and endurance of the new enterprise, while Ernest himself was looking for new horizons and new opportunities at home and abroad, creating, where necessary, new jobs to be filled by the very many capable people he knew he could call upon. Unlike many great captains of industry, lacking foresight and vision, he knew how to find the right man for the right job.

At the height of fame and fortune, great industrialists like to turn to the Arts and patronage: they endow, they found and they buy. Their collections usually demonstrate great flair for investment rather than personal artistic taste. What are their real motivations?

It would appear that Ernest Solvay was not particularly attracted to painting, writing or music. He was more inspired by science and loved Nature. It has been said that only the beauty of his garden touched him. He was an observer and a thinker, very sensitive to the social climate of his times. He strove hard to improve conditions, not only by suggestions which were often derided by those who read or heard them, but also by improvements in his own factories. This industrial genius's moral,

Ernest Solvay, painting by Émile Wauters.

11

Ernest Solvay
1863 - 1922

Armand Solvay
1922 - 1930

Louis Solvay
1931 - 1947

Ernest-John Solvay
1947 - 1963

René Boël
1964 - 1971

Jacques Solvay
1971

Daniel Janssen
1986

Solvay & Cie's seven chairmen.
In the background, the Couillet plant where the Solvays' industrial adventure was born.

political, social and economic vision was unusual for the times and made him a leading figure in the second half of the 19th century, a haven for the great owners of coal-mines, steel and glass works, etc. Most of them did not have this far-sighted vision or not the means for generosity. Did they have the slightest inkling that paradise would be lost forever if the under-privileged were never to be allowed to share in it? They were astute, daring and able but they lacked Ernest Solvay's caring attitute which he kept hidden under a somewhat cold exterior. He did not just satisfy himself with the discovery of the production method for sodium carbonate from salt, ammonia and carbon dioxide, applying for a patent on April 15, 1861 but worked constantly for better conditions for all those employed in his factories, including the humblest.

His successors have inherited his business acumen and his constant concern to improve the personnel's working and living conditions. They have fought many battles to develop, gain a reputation, adjust and survive. It must be clearly said that all these battles were victoriously won. An empire's longevity is determined by the personal qualities of its heirs.

P A R T   O N E

ERNEST SOLVAY'S CAREER

I. THE EARLY YEARS

Exceptional people are nearly always disconcerting. The person whose biography we are about to write was a discoverer, an industrialist, a Senator, a Minister of State, a Doctor Honoris Causa of the Université Libre de Bruxelles (Free University of Brussels in Belgium) and the Université de Genève (University of Geneva in Switzerland), a corresponding member of the Institut de France and Berlin's Academy of Science (West Germany). He enjoyed good health at an age when others begin to lose it, dying much older than all his doctors had predicted. Nature gave him time to fulfil his life's work and he died knowing that what he had achieved through his intelligence and determination would not disappear once he was gone.

*

*   *

April 16, 1838: birth of Ernest Solvay; Belgium is still in its infancy. The Solvay family has chosen to settle in a small village in southern Belgium (the Walloon region) with the slightly curious and funny name of Rebecq-Rognon (*), not far from Tubize, in fact closer to Tubize than to Nivelles where Ernest's father, Alexandre Solvay, was to be the Vice-Chairman of the local Chamber of Commerce. The countryside is pleasant, rolling and peaceful; to the South, the industrial belt — the Borinage region — and the black seams of the coal mines.

Alexandre Solvay was a quarry-master and salt maker, that is to say he refined salt, the refinery being installed in the family home. In addition, he was a wholesaler for oil, soap and colonial supplies. All these goods were imported from abroad, showing how this provincial family background was already open to the outside world and highlighting, from the outset, the paradox of launching a major industry based on the one natural resource this local inhabitant's country did not possess: salt. There are signs which have to be acknowledged — we know now the role that salt was to play in Ernest Solvay's life.

He could very well have come across it along the way but this was not to be — it was already present very early on in his life.

(*) Translator note: «rognon» means «kidney».

*Adèle and
Alexandre Solvay,
Ernest's parents.*

These are rather theatrical words for a totally untheatrical and unartistic family. However, family background does not get in the way of a dream and a scientist is per se a dreamer. Things came to his mind which no one else would think of. Does this mean that Ernest Solvay could have been a writer, painter or composer? Why not — his inner demons, though, pushed him to invent. His parents had the same hopes as other parents for their sons: good schools and a good job with the prospect of becoming Vice-Chairman of the Nivelles Chamber of Commerce like his father, why maybe even the Chairmanship.

Ernest Solvay was a good student but was never to go to university. This scholar was not the product of one of the prestigious schools. Personality, inventive genius and perseverance are not acquired in university lecture halls, although they are not frowned upon by such institutions. With all his personal qualities, Ernest would most certainly have received high honors from the Université de Liège (Belgium) where his parents had intended sending him and where quite possibly he would have stayed. This was not to be and in any event, a boy like him, unable to keep still for very long, would have been stifled by the rigid teaching, even though he would have left his mark on his own pupils. He always preferred a brush with reality rather than a safe position in an ivory tower.

Due to poor health, his *Alma mater* lost a precious recruit but Science gained a scholar and the World, a benefactor. The studious adolescent must have been disheartened at having to give up his studies and for the rest of his life, he regretted not having a degree in engineering. He had a very great knowledge of the field where others preferred to limit themselves to lecture halls and worn-out books. Pasteur was not a doctor either.

Ernest and his brother Alfred, born two years later on July 1, 1840 and who had a very much shorter life, dying in Nice on January 23, 1894, went to the village primary school in Rebecq. The older boy was high-spirited and full of vitality, joking and wrestling with his school friends, playing a game of «balle pelote» — a popular game in the region. The younger brother, however, was a quiet, placid child and many years later, this level-headedness was to be of great service to Ernest.

Ernest no doubt inherited his father's high spirits (who had a great passion for horse-racing), whereas Alfred was more like his mother of whom not much is known; yet she brought up two sons and three daughters who seem to have been a mischievous

Ernest's birthplace in Rebecq.

20

lot. Despite the usual teasing between the brothers and sisters, the Solvay's were a very closely-knit family and they remained so until the end. Kindness and generosity were common to them all.

With the exception of the eldest son and the youngest daughter, all the names of the Solvay family began with the first letter of the alphabet: Alexandre married Adèle Hulin. Three of their children were called Aurélie, Alfred and Alfonsa. There were still many names beginning with A — why did they decide on Ernest and Elisa?

The father liked to philosophise, a trait his eldest son inherited, and published a collection of his thoughts. For instance, he liked to say «How many people would remain silent if they were prohibited from saying good of themselves and bad of others.» He taught his children to be true to themselves, once they had carried out their duties and not to concern themselves unduly with other people's opinions of them.

Of the two boys, Ernest was the more intelligent but without Alfred, he would have just been an inventor. What would he have achieved without him? The younger brother fought his battles in obscurity since he did not like centre stage but his tenacity helped to overcome the disappointments of the early years. Alfred had the knack of minimizing failure and emphasizing success. They had been working together for 15 years when Ernest wrote him the following passage: *I had become totally identified with my process and could not be without it, you had become identified with me, like a devoted brother but you never, never suffered a moment's despair ... Since we needed each other to be successful, we developed the process together and it truly belongs to both of us: it is the bi-Solvay process.*

At that time, the two brothers need not have doubted their success. They were already famous but seventeen years later, Ernest was crushed by the death of the brother who had given up his job with a shipping agent to answer his brother's call preferring the unknown to a safe future. Ernest shook him by the shoulders, repeating over and over again «Tell me, why have you left me?»

From the village primary school, Ernest went on to secondary school in Malonne. The Brothers of Christian Doctrine were well-known for their excellent teaching and students came from far and wide. It was there that Ernest discovered his real passion, chemistry. He was always questioning his teachers and spent much time studying and reading, even hiding his lamp under the blankets. It was there that he had the misfortune of catching cold but still insisted on continuing. He was not only determined but also obstinate, finally taking to his bed with a serious case of pleurisy.

At the time, this illness inspired fear and trembling. The Solvays had decided that after Malonne, their son would go on to higher education. They knew he had the ability, his room was already like a real laboratory, but the doctors advised strenuously against it, and so Ernest returned to Rebecq. He was sixteen years old and would not return to school again or attend university. He would educate himself, keeping a picture by his bedside, inset with the portraits of all the great scholars of the times.

Out of necessity, his years of study were solitary years, but which did not displease him. Ernest experimented and learned to count only on his own experience and not on other people's work. He made his mistakes but also gained in originality and independence of judgement. Later on, everyone would know that he only relied on his own way of doing things and was born obstinate. Would he have persevered had he not been born with inner resources which he knew he could not leave untapped? Had he been in better health, he may well have had the same personality but he would surely have learned that inventions do not come out of thin air.

After a short spell spent with his brother in Antwerp working for a merchant, Ernest was called upon to assist his Uncle Semet who was the director of a gas plant in Saint-Josse-ten-Node, a district of Brussels. He was to study and find a solution to the problems of processing ammonia liquor. After dealing with salt at his father's, he was now to discover ammonia at his uncle's. These two substances were to become the vital elements of his life as a scientist and inventor. Incidentally, his Uncle Semet had dealt with the development of coke ovens which were built and used in the United States and which were sold under the name of «Production of Semet-Solvay coke ovens». His descendants remained connected to the company that the young Ernest had, as yet, not dreamed of launching.

At the time — 1860 — knowledge of ammonia was still very sketchy. Uncle Semet had appointed his young nephew to the position of assistant-director of his factory but this grand title was not an invitation to idleness. He intended young Ernest to work hard and *he* needed no reminding. Day after day, he worked on the purification and scrubbing of the gas, on the extraction and

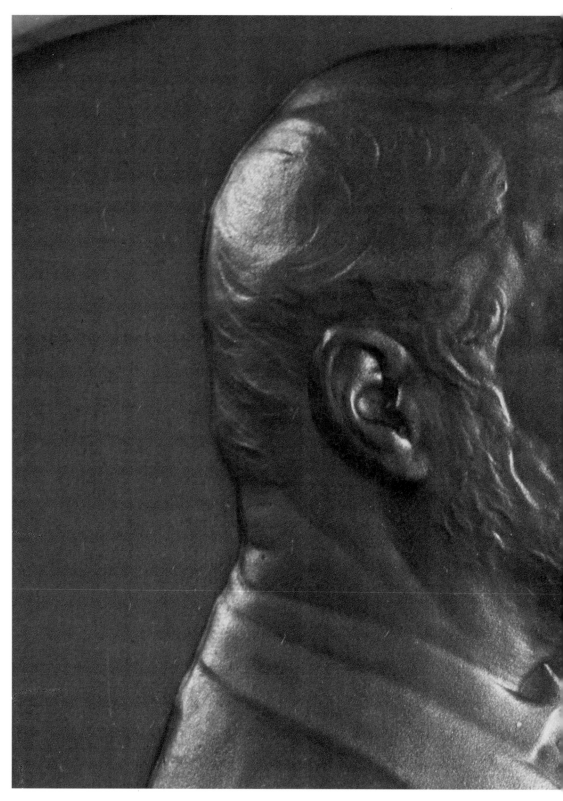

Ernest and Alfred Solvay.

concentration of the ammonia liquor, and on tar separation and the pressure regulation of the gas. A whole new area opened up before him for the design of new apparatus, giving his inventive genius free reign and the impetus to carry on with his experiments and chemical research.

Chance gave him a helping hand. He collected ammonia gas and carbon dioxide in salt water and not, as usual, in ordinary

Ernest Solvay in 1860.

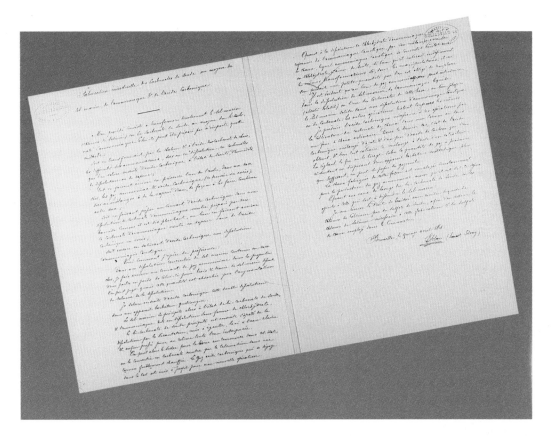

Ernest Solvay's first patent, April 15, 1861.

water. He shook the mixture and suddenly he realized what had happened. The liquid had thickened — a reaction had occured. The white precipitate was, in fact, sodium bicarbonate.

Had he not been Ernest Solvay, he would have been happy just to note the chemical results, but he realized that this was an industrial process and begun to work out calculations. The soda still cost 700 francs a ton which was little compared with previous prices but was still high considering that it could be produced much more cheaply by a more efficient method. According to his calculations, the price could fall to about 175 or even 150 francs, as long as all the ammonia was extracted. This was certainly not impossible, quite on the contrary. He talked to his uncle who was very interested and encouraged him in his research, sensing that this might be a way of making good use of the ammonia liquor which had, up to now, been considered as a fairly worthless by-product from gas production, its pure ammonia content being insignificant to be of any real commercial interest. Using a method he had invented, Ernest Solvay intended to extract the ammonia and then concentrate the solution by heating it and distilling it with lime.

On April 15, 1861, he decided to apply for his patent, the first of a very long list. The title read as follows: — *Industrial Production of sodium carbonate, using salt, ammonia and carbon dioxide*. He thought that he had broken new ground. His predecessors had all failed in their attempts at industrial production of the same method.

II. THE OBSTACLES

The Solvay name is so closely linked to soda that we should perhaps take a closer look at its composition.

The dictionary gives two definitions under the heading *soda*:
1. soda from the latin word *soda*, (Bot) a plant species of the *chenopodiceae* family from which sodium carbonate used to be extracted.
2. soda (as 1. above) (Chem.) term describing sodium hydroxide (*caustic soda*) or sodium carbonate (*soda crystals*).

We shall start with the plant and its uses. The plant, which grows in salt planes and contains soda, is called «salsola» (saltwort) or «alkali» which is an Arabic word used to refer to all substances with basic propriety. There are very big salt deposits in the world and the term «volatile alkali» refers to nothing other than ammonia. Now that this basic information has been given, we can continue with our story.

This book is not intended as a scientific or technical reference document and so we shall only give a brief description of the history of alkali, soda and ammonia, concerning their uses in antiquity up to the end of the 18th century. During early Antiquity, housewives did their washing with the ashes from the alcaline plant. This was hung over the washing and hot water was then poured over it extracting the ammonia which was then used to do the washing. The Assyrians used alkali as a medicinal remedy in such widely different illnesses as jaundice, pleurisy and kidney ailments.

Soda can be found in the ashes of various plants. What Herodotus called *nitron* in Greek (and which we know as natron) was in fact a compound of natural sodium carbonate and bicarbonate, found in the Natron Wadi in Egypt. It was used in the dyeing of fabrics, in the production of glass, for the washing and bleaching of textiles and in the production of soap.

We shall not go any further, suffice it to say that man had discovered alkali and its many uses: ashes for washing, the plant for medicinal purposes, caustic alkali extracted from the ashes and oil added to produce soap. When mixed with sand and submitted to high temperatures, it produced glass. According to Pline, it was also used for embalming, when mixed with incense. This is, however, not entirely certain.

The various uses of alkali changed very little until the arrival of man-made soda which became increasingly necessary. Production of low-grade (15%) soda from the saltwort plant had become insufficient. One new endeavor was to increase the soda content by adding calcined seaweed. Imported from Spain or Brittany, these quantities of soda were insufficient to provide the impetus for real industrial expansion. In 1736, Duhamel Dumonceau demonstrated that soda and salt had the same basic structure and the research which followed stemmed from this discovery. In 1776, the French Academy of Sciences, in Paris, launched a competition, endowed with 2400 francs in prize money which was *to be given to the scientist who discovered the simplest and cheapest method for the industrial separation of salt and the extraction of alkali, in its purest form, free from any acid or neutral compound elements and for no higher price than that which is obtained with the use of the best foreign soda.*

The winner was to be Nicolas Leblanc of whom Ernest Solvay spoke very highly more than once and who was his great predecessor. Unfortunately, Leblanc was haunted by fate — a combination of uncertainty of the times and mean quibbling. In despair, he shot himself in 1805.

Leblanc discovered the method for transforming salt into soda as one may read on the plaque of his statue which was erected in 1886 in the courtyard of the «Conservatoire des Arts et Métiers» (Museum and College of Higher Technology for training students in the application of science to industry) in Paris. Unfortunately, during the Revolution and due to the stupidity of the Committee for Public Safety which had cancelled all the patents, Leblanc's discovery crossed the Channel and he was expelled from his own factory. What was his method? Salt was treated with sulfuric acid producing sodium sulfate and hydrochloric acid. The sodium sulfate was then treated with chalk and carbon giving off sodium carbonate and also two other very unpleasant by-products: foul-smelling sulfuric ashes (sodium sulfide) and toxic carbon monoxide. However, the Chairmen of the Committee for Public Safety praised this invention in the following words: *We believe that this method (invented by citizen Leblanc) may very easily be adopted since its basic element is most widely found. In addition, it has the advantage of enabling the soda to be put on the market in its raw state, that it closely resembles the imported soda to which we have been accustomed for many years and finally, that it may be used, without further leaching, for washing, glass- and soap-*

making. This method being based on the use of sulfuric acid, the resulting hydrochloric acid combines, in that state of purity, to produce sal ammoniac.

This was all very fine and ought to have convinced the entire Committee for Public Safety. They were convinced but an obsession with principles, i.e. the banning of personal property, won the day. As always, there was a momentary respite, and Leblanc multiplied his efforts at recovering his factory and the money which he had been promised as national reward. Of the original sum of three thousand francs, he only received six hundred and when his factory was finally handed back to him (after six years and nine months of inactivity), not much was left. On top of it all, his method had become public property — it was used in Marseille, Lille and abroad to produce soda and supply soap factories, glass-works, dyers and bleaching houses. No matter how much Leblanc called for justice, he was never to be given satisfaction; quite on the contrary, all his petitions were met with endless procrastination. Finally, weary and disgusted, he took his

Soda production from the alkali plant.

own life. In other circumstances, however, he would have known fame and fortune.

Leblanc had a special place in Solvay's heart, due to his trials and tribulations. He, too, had had to struggle and strive in order to achieve his aims and to be able to continue his endeavors. He knew that he had been successful and that he had won the battle. Leblanc, on the other hand, acknowledged defeat by committing suicide.

Leblanc and Solvay had other points in common such as little formal education, an inquiring mind and some major discoveries. Leblanc's name is only known by specialists, whereas Solvay's is a household name. This industry which was to be superseded by Solvay's discovery, would never have existed without Leblanc's contribution.

Had Leblanc's patent been kept secret, France would have controlled the chemical industry which already existed in Great Britain where it had undergone spectacular development, especially towards the 1850's. This development was linked to cotton which required vast quantities of soda and chlorine, used in the bleaching process. The sulfuric acid which was necessary in the production of Leblanc's soda was quite easily produced and the process itself absorbed increasing amounts of sulfuric acid, giving off great quantities of hydrochloric acid which were later converted into chlorine and used in bleaching powder (chloride of lime), bleach and disinfectant (Javel water), etc. All types of industries based on products and by-products from Leblanc's discovery became established, such as glue and gelatine factories, glass-works, soap factories and paper mills. Towards the middle of the 19th century, there were 130 factories in England alone, producing soda using the Leblanc method.

The products' cost price was considerably increased due to the series of high-temperature operations which this method required. In addition, the sodium content was never higher than 40% and further refining had to be carried out, adding extra expenses. Although there had been a sharp fall in prices since the early 1800's, a ton of soda still sold for 700 francs. Ernest Solvay's method had the advantage of obtaining a reaction at very low temperatures. By extracting all the ammonia, which was relatively easy, he was sure that he could bring the price down even further, to 175 or even 150 francs per ton, as we have already mentioned. This is why he filed an application for his first patent, encouraged by his uncle who as stated above, hoped to make

1. Adoration of natron, a fresco from 19th Dynasty. Natron was made from carbonate and sodium bicarbonate and was found in the Natrum Wady in Egypt.

2. Natron was used to purify corpses for embalming. Archaic Period. The Hildesheim Museum.

3. Bleaching of laundry. Thebes. Fresco from 19th Dynasty.
4. The salt wort plant. In Antiquity, the most common source of soda was the ashes from various plants.
5. The god Anubis, symbolizing embalmers, purifies a corpse with natron. New Empire, Cairo Museum.

good use of the ammonia liquor which was a dangerous by-product from gas production.

My method consists in using bicarbonate of ammonia for the immediate conversion of salt — i.e. sodium chloride — into bicarbonate of soda — signed Ernest Solvay. Had he continued his studies — which he was not able to due to poor health — he would have learned that what he believed to be a new process, had in fact been discovered, fifty years before, by the French physicist Augustin Fresnel. Any one other than Ernest Solvay would no doubt have given up but illness had tempered his personality. Moreover, he recognized that his method was superior to Leblanc's, although this had also been remarkable. The production of carbonate of sodium not only required very high temperatures but also entailed the stocking of nauseating sulfuric ashes (sodium suflide) which give off hydrochloric acid and

1

2

3

4

5

carbon monoxide, both very dangerous gases for the human lung as well as for the British lawn. The use of the Solvay method, on the other hand, meant that the chlorine produced from the salt stayed in the solution and combined with the calcium to produce soluble calcium chloride, doing away with the very high temperatures which were previously necessary. In addition, the ammonia which was the basis of the production method was recovered.

Ernest Solvay was right in being stubborn and persistent and he was sufficiently intelligent to know how to listen to people. He had very often been shown the door by various Belgian industrialists but was finally persuaded by his father's best friend, Gustave Sabatier, to go and see Eudore Pirmez, a lawyer living in Charleroi who told him «to verify the authenticity of his patent, in order to establish its worth and to be able to prove it». At that time, Belgian patents were given without any prior examination, the authors being held responsible.

The company's birthplace, the Couillet plant (Belgium), in 1877, i.e. 12 years after its creation.

It was in this way that he learned that he was fifty years too late — this chemical reaction, already experimented with in England, France, Germany and Italy, had been abandoned since it cost more than it yielded.

Augustin Fresnel, the original inventor in 1811 of this method and who also discovered the theory of undulatory light, had realized the importance of his discovery; yet, the Leblanc process was widely acclaimed and gained general acceptance. Moreover, Fresnel had not developed a process for recovering ammonia which was at the time a scarce and expensive substance. The method's simplicity greatly impressed the other scientists, such as for instance Dyar and Hemming in England. An industrialist by the name of Sheridan Muspradt built a factory in Newton with a view to exploiting this new method but two years later after having spent 8000 pounds sterling, he decided to cut his losses. Due to important losses of ammonia and excessive production

costs, the process was considered less efficient than Leblanc's which remained the only one still in the running after the many disappointments encountered in Germany, Austria and Great Britain. In 1854 in Puteaux, two French engineers, Schloesing and Rolland had patented various equipment designed to improve the ammonia's chemical reaction and decided to try their luck, hoping to find fame and fortune. Despite the superiority of their method, based on the continuous process which Solvay had also used, despite proper organization and experience, they met the

Dyers. 15th century. Alkali extracted from the plant is added to the dye as a fixing agent in wool dying.
The British Museum, London, Great Britain.

same fate as their predecessors and were finally forced to close their factory after only four years of production which swallowed up their entire capital of 1.5 million francs.

Ernest and Alfred (having returned at Ernest's request from Hull, England, where he was undergoing business training and subsequently Louis-Philippe Acheroy, an old school-friend from the Rebecq years and who originally had thought of going into

Statue of Nicolas Leblanc (1742 - 1806), the inventor of the first industrial production method for sodium carbonate (1790).

the priesthood — later, Ernest was to take on Prosper Hanrez, founder of the Dombasle factory, Edouard Hannon, Edgar Hulin and Louis Semet) were much too hardened to be affected by earlier failures. On the contrary, this only encouraged them. Specialists' reactions to their project and initial findings which had already cost them 35000 francs, varied from blatant scepticism, kind encouragement to occasionally undisguised interest. Ernest was congratulated on the vertical design of his equipment which had previously been arranged horizontally and which helped to accelerate a very slow process. However, when he informed the interested parties that he intended producing soda at less than 150 francs per ton, they laughed at him, never thinking that even at 90 francs per ton it would still make a profit! The most optimistic among them were talking of 250 francs. Others, like the Saint-Gobain company to whom the two brothers had offered involvement in their project, had declined the invitation. Each of the brothers' endeavors brought new hope, only to be cruelly shattered. Nothing but negative answers can finally break a person's will.

Yet, Eudore Pirmez never-failingly encouraged them by saying in essence «You are on the right road, you must not give up. Would so many scientists have spent so much time and money on the development of this method if it were of no value whatsoever?» These words of encouragement led the Solvays to set up their company — Solvay & Cie. — on December 26, 1863 under a limited partnership with a capital of 136000 francs, 34000 of which represented the brothers' equipment, inventions and work and the remainder being provided by the investors sitting on the company's Supervisory Board.

The Articles of Incorporation were signed before the Notary Vandam in Charleroi. The acting partners were Ernest and Alfred Solvay, the company's sleeping partners were three members of the House of Representatives: Guillaume Nélis, Eudore Pirmez and Gustave Sabatier to whom one must add the names of Léonard Pirmez and Miss Hyacinthe Pirmez, members of Deputy Eudore Pirmez' family, and Valentin Lambert, his father-in-law. It is thus that Eudore Pirmez, lawyer and friend in need, not only gave Ernest and his younger brother sound advice and encouragement but also decided to help them financially and even to find three other investors who were members of his own family. He and Gustave Sabatier also involved one of their parliamentary colleagues by the name of Guillaume Nélis. The Articles stipulated that Ernest would only receive his salary after the investors had been paid 8% of their original investment and after Alfred had received his annual salary of 2500 francs.

Alfred who had moved to Couillet which was the site chosen for the factory, just south of Charleroi, wrote to his brother on March 14, 1864: *I have laid the foundation stone for the new factory. May it be the bedrock of a steady and prosperous new enterprise which will reward you, Ernest, for all your trials and tribulations and insomnia and for all that you have endured for the family and especially for me. I hope to be worthy of this position and should the case arise, be able to manage the company in a manner worthy of you. On thinking of all this, I cannot but shed a few tears ... of happiness rather than sadness.*

While Alfred was directing the construction of the factory, Ernest was still employed at his uncle Semet's Saint-Josse gas plant. However, he made frequent visits to Couillet, so frequent that his uncle was annoyed with him. Ernest finally handed in his resignation on August 14, 1865, the day before the birth of Ernest's second child.

At Couillet, Ernest took on many jobs such as engineer, foreman, draughtsman, fitter, etc., while Alfred was the company's accountant, cashier, storekeeper, dispatcher and loader. Both were helped in their tasks by Louis-Philippe Acheroy. They had very little respite from all their activities, as Ernest himself explained: «The uphill battle began in 1865 when the factory started up, requiring constant perfecting of the equipment. We also had a series of accidents, all part and parcel of a new industrial production method.

This was the difficult road we had to follow and had I not had Alfred Solvay, my devoted assistant, I am certain I should have given up.»

Alfred was the company's managing director until his death. Founder and director of the Couillet plant, he returned to Brussels in 1879 to devote his energies to the management of the expanding group. He traveled the world, studying the deposits of natural resources as well as possible industrial sites and both the needs and market openings of the countries visited. His business acumen, together with sound judgement, his special skills, his foresight and his common sense were to be determining factors in Ernest's expansion of the company.

At that time, any suggestion that the Leblanc empire was under attack would have met with a thin smile or a shrug of the

At left:
salt recovery:
A. The sea
B. Pool
C. Dam
D. Trenches
E. Salt
concentration ponds
F. Rake
G. Spade

Opposite page:
Above:
General view of the
manual salt
recovery at Solvay's
Esnisa site in Brazil.
Below:
On the same site,
automation of the
salt recovery and
conveyor belt
transportation.

41

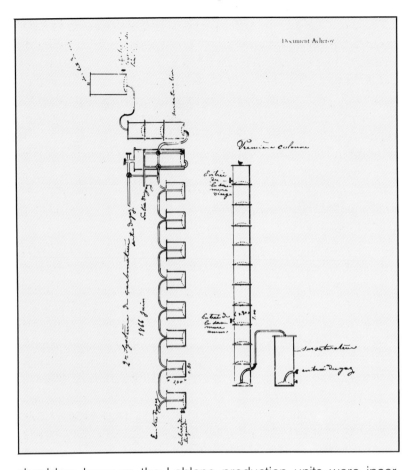

Ernest Solvay invented a system of columns which considerably improved the chemical reaction during the production of sodium carbonate.

shoulders because the Leblanc production units were incorporated into very well-established chemical plants for the production of the following: sulfuric, nitric and hydrochloric acid, soda, chlorinated lime, chlorites, etc. What were the Solvays thinking of when they launched their bid? Had they forgotten Schloesing and Rolland's recent failure? They had fully understood the soda industry's need for the ammonia process, writing in their memoirs: *The ammonia process consists in making bicarbonate of ammonia react with the salt solution. Bicarbonate of soda is produced by double exchange and is precipitated into a fine powder — only solid salt crystals, hydrochloride and ammonia bicarbonate remain. Instead of using ready-made bicarbonate, one may dissolve ammonia in salt solution and saturate the carbonic acid solution. This is the most important step. Those that follow filter, wash and calcinate the sodium bicarbonate precipitate producing neutral carbonate and carbonic acid and finally treat the filtered solutions to recover the ammonia.*

Then why give up? *Because the Puteaux factory was only*

built to carry out experiments and was not meant, due to its loca-tion and the need for equipment, to produce soda at profitable prices. In the words of Schloesing and Rolland, we thought we had achieved our goal and that the factory had thus no further purpose. In fact, they had met with a serious problem from the Internal Revenu Service (I.R.S.). This department demanded the rights on all the salt solution delivered to the factory and since the ammonia process lost one third of its salt content in the pro-cess, this meant that 18 francs per 100 kgs of carbonate were lost in profits (180 kgs of salt were needed to produce 100 kgs of carbonate of soda). The profit margin was too narrow to enable them to carry on and in all events they did not wish to do so. In Belgium, the salt levy was finally abolished in 1862 thanks to the efforts of Nélis and Sabatier who were both Congressmen and were acting on the advice of Eudore Pirmez. Schloesing and Rolland were both scientists and were not prepared for all the practical challenges. Ernest Solvay had faith in his inner resources as well as in the new theories he was applying. He could also count on his brother's organizational skills and on the full sup-port of his entire family. These synergies could only lead to success.

However, this success was to be seriously jeopardized. While the two brothers and their foreman were carrying out repairs without initially stopping the machine, the three men were over-come by gas fumes and collapsed, unconscious. But for a workman's chance arrival on the scene, dragging the men to the door and to fresh air, Ernest would have died at the age of 24, his brother at 22 and the Solvays' story would have ended then and there.

III. SUCCESS

Success was near, without as yet being fully attained. The Couillet plant, later to be known as the «mother plant», was ready to start production at the end of 1864. At the beginning of that year, Ernest Solvay had written to the Ministry of Public Works: *«We, the undersigned, Solvay & Cie, having decided to erect a large factory at Couillet for the production of soda salt, humbly request your permission to link our factory directly up to the State railway system... We feel duty bound to inform the Minister that we shall be moving between 18 and 20 tons of raw material and about 5 tons of finished products — i.e. a total load of between 23 and 25 tons per 24 hour period.»*

There were several reasons why Ernest Solvay had chosen this particular site for his first Belgian factory: firstly, he did not wish to move away from his investors, the Pirmez family who lived in Charleroi; secondly, he wished to be in close proximity to a ready source of labor which was very abundant in this industrial region. He also wanted to have easy access to good transport facilities such as the river Sambre and a rail link for transport of salt to, and soda from, the factory; finally, he needed to have a steady supply of coal, ammonia liquor and calcium carbonate which were all readily available due to the proximity of coal mines, gas plants and the local limestone quarries. The only negative aspect of the Couillet site was that there was no local salt mine, but then there is not a single such mine in all of Belgium.

In his letter to the Minister, the young industrialist showed great optimism. Reality was to outstrip all his forecasts but when? He spent night and day testing the apparatus, replacing faulty parts. His brother and he even spent New Year's Day of 1865 working at the factory. When they finally started production, they only managed to produce 600 to 800 kgs a day. Where were all the promised tons? A little later, production had reached one ton but with great difficulty and the factory's financial situation had become worrisome. The brothers were seriously overdrawn at the bank and a ominous crack had developed in what the brothers termed the main apparatus. Due to their meager finances, they were only able to carry out make-shift repairs which did not withstand for long.

Liquidation appeared inevitable. Eudore Pirmez felt unable

to invest any further family funds in the project and set about finding Alfred and Ernest alternative employment, Ernest being granted the La Louvière (Belgium) agency of the Banque Nationale. A family council was held in Rebecq on October 29, 1863 at which the word «bankruptcy» was mentioned, for the first and last time. For not only did the entire Solvay family stand firmly behind the brothers, the investors gave renewed support for the further attempts at increased production. The Solvays' parents found an extra 40000 francs and the shareholders provided the money for the most urgent repairs and improvements. That was about the full extent of everyone's ability and the last remaining problems were to be solved and the ammonia process used in the industrial production of soda would finally see the day.

The young Ernest Solvay.

A change in fortunes was apparent! Production increased little by little; from 1 1/2 tons per day produced on that decisive day of 1866, it increased to 3 tons by the following year. The two brothers could be well satisfied but those using the Leblanc process had not yet changed attitudes. They were producing 1000 times more in 1866 and still 175 times more in 1869 than the Solvays and kept up the fight to maintain their leading position. They had experience and did not lack the resources. They did not shy away from using pyrites, increasing the volume of the lead chambers or improving production conditions to such an extent that the price of sulfuric acid registered a spectacular fall.

This drop in price might very well not have occurred had the Solvay process not made its appearance on the market. Thanks to the battle between the supporters of the two methods which finally saw the new-comer win, sulfuric acid was to be used in the treatment of natural and mineral phosphates and was to have a positive effect on agriculture; cereal yields were to increase, leading to cheaper bread. This can probably not be ascribed solely to the Solvay process — a range of parallel developments was no doubt involved. However, thanks to Solvay, the chemical industry's overall possibilities were to be increased and developed.

It is quite clear that Solvay himself understood the importance of this development. A visionary is not limited to the present. By wanting to give his process the widest applications possible, Solvay did not deviate from his chosen course. Since his discovery of producing soda from ammonia, he had not stopped being an inventor and continued working on improvements for his apparatus, devising what has since been called the «Solvay column» which is used in most soda works around the world.

What needed doing to bring about cheaper production costs? The answer was cheaper fuel and to that end, it was vital to recover the ammonia by increasing its absorption efficiency. Solvay's predecessors had used vessels with agitators. Schloesing and Rolland had designed an absorber into which the salt solution, ammonia and carbonic acid were added, filtering through a series of horizontal cylinders called absorbers which were mounted in cascade formation and linked together by large lateral tubes, traversed by agitators and in which the liquids and gases were in counter-flow. Ernest Solvay used this method until 1869 at which time he adopted the idea of a vertical tower formation with mounted cast-iron cylinders into which the carbonic acid was injected from below at a pressure of several atmospheres, while the ammonia brine solution flowed through from above. Thanks to this apparatus which was now vertical (previously it had been arranged horizontally) with its columns sometimes well over 10 meters in height (about 33 ft), the ammonia liquor and the gas came into close contact and the violent agitation arising out of the gas's bubbling action facilitated its absorption by the solution. At the Solvay plant, total reaction time was 5 hours, elsewhere it took two to three times as long.

The year 1869 was a watershed. From then on, the Solvay process gained ground even if outright victory had not yet been achieved. Production increased, the Couillet plant was expanded and a new factor, twice as important as the first one, came into play.

An enormous effort had been made and considerable financial risks had been taken and the founders had no intention of stopping now that everything was running fairly smoothly. They might very well have been able to realize their investment by selling off the company and the new production method but such an idea never entered Ernest's thoughts. From then on, he was already considering transforming his small production company, located on the edge of Charleroi's industrial bassin, into an international group with wide-ranging ambitions.

In comparison with the Leblanc process, the Solvays had proved the economic superiority of their production method. The principal natural resource, salt, was cheap; the only problem was that it had to be imported from afar. In addition, the transport costs for soda made it difficult to supply the entire European market from one production site. Protectionism practiced by the major consumer countries also had to be taken into consideration. The superiority of the Solvay process could only be fully realized through the setting-up of a European network of soda works located in close proximity to salt deposits and within easy reach of the ready markets. Ernest Solvay knew that the Leblanc process would eventually fall into disuse and he wished to prepare and ensure the company's future.

He was soon to set up companies in those countries where there were salt and limestone deposits. He established a survey of the state of European salt deposits and his methodical mind could also be seen to be at work in the strict supervision and monitoring of operations: every hour, the solutions and gases were chemically analysed and heat, pressure and flux readings were taken; this information was then logged on a chart next to each apparatus. Similar information was gathered by the factory's laboratory technicians and the two sets of information were carefully studied and compared; consumption rates of raw materials were monitored in order to determine the company's production strategy and also to take note of those areas requiring improvement.

Solvay's first foreign factory was built in 1874 in Dombasle-sur-Meurthe in France's Lorraine region, since there were subterranean salt deposits nearby. Factories in Great Britain, Austria, Germany and Russia followed within the next 10 years and were to adopt the same flow charts as had already been adopted by the original factory in Couillet. Every month, this information was transmitted to the company's headquarters in Brussels where it was analysed and used to make comparisons before sending off the appropriate instructions to the various factories. Once a year, each soda factory's yields were examined by the central management's technical division which would then advise on improvements to be carried out. Central management was set up in 1883 in the rue du Prince Albert in Ixelles (a district of Brussels) where it is still located, the present buildings having been extended on several occasions. It was and still is the company's decision-making center, where strategy is determined. The various charts, devised by Ernest Solvay and now know as «production charts», are still in use today.

The management center has, from the outset, been the group's nerve center, ensuring collection of the information from the various production units, its processing and subsequent communication, in the industry's special jargon, to all the various branches within the group. The Solvay process being the first efficient industrial application of a well-known chemical reaction, it was useless to count solely on the patents for industrial protection. Ernest Solvay, in addition, encouraged the use of a secret weapon: all the documents were rendered illegible to the layman by replacing the key-words with signs and the use of a specially invented language.

This policy, strangely enough, cemented the group's unity, the executives taking pride in belonging to an international inner circle. Such spontaneous solidarity was not only to be seen in the technical divisions but very quickly reached all the other areas of the company. This policy has its origins in the 19th century and survived the two world wars; it is still alive and well today, being considered as normal practice within the group. Yet, the

In 1883,
the Company's
Central
Administration was
installed in the Rue
du Prince Albert,
Brussels, Belgium.

outside world has the impression of a very closed organization, jealously retaining its own specificity. However, the company's policy of readily providing information concerning all areas of its activities — with the exception of production secrets and strategy — does not justify this opinion.

Returning to Ernest Solvay's methodical approach, he applied it to all the tests carried out on new apparatus, and to any new production method. Tests were always made in several factories at the same time and in so doing information received from different sources enabled him to make a decision based on established facts. This procedure was and still is one of the main reasons for the Solvay brothers' success. Before the introduction of this procedure, it was the foreman's skill, sometimes his flair, which was of vital importance even when the results were chemically analysed to ensure the product's quality. The Solvays, however, introduced repeated monitoring during production which enabled timely correction of errors and/or deficiencies.

This methodical and careful approach was also reflected in the choice of production sites. Ernest and Alfred Solvay pored over the maps, locating the most suitable sites regarding easy supply of raw materials at the best prices. These possible sites were then inspected by the Solvays or by their assistants. Their competitors showed neither the boldness nor the mobility and the brothers' pioneering spirit has been handed down to later generations, becoming a Solvay family trait.

Ludwig Mond, a German chemist and the director of a British soda works whose production was based on the Leblanc method with a yearly capacity of 40000 tons of soda, observed these two young Belgians and was greatly impressed by their energy and initiative. He was convinced he could reach 80000, possibly even 100000 tons using their production process and informed Ernest Solvay to this effect. The two men met and later finalized their discussions with an agreement. The date — April 1872.

The 1870 Franco-Prussian War had delayed the construction of the soda works at Dombasle which was finished in 1874. Further plants were built at an ever-increasing pace and the next one to be built in France was at Giraud, in the Bouches-du-Rhône. Ernest Solvay set up the Deutsche Solvay-Werke (Germany) in 1883 and launched the construction of the Bernburg, Wyhlen (Grand Duchy of Bade, now Bade Land) and Sarralbe factories, the latter being located in the annexed Lorraine. The subsidiary Lubimoff-Solvay started the soda works at Bereznicki and the

Ebenseer Solvay-Werke (Austro-Hungary) were set up and inaugurated the Ebensee factory. Further soda works were built in Yugoslavia (formerly Lukavac), at Ocna (a region which was later to be annexed by Romania) and at Podgorze (which subsequently became Polish). Ernest Solvay had crisscrossed Europe, creating a spider's web of interconnecting industries. In England, his agreement with Mond led to the setting-up of the Brunner-Mond company which erected the Northwich in 1873 and later the Sandbach, Middlewich and Lostock soda works, with the British Empire as their field of action. These early developments were later to be the cornerstone of the Imperial Chemical Industries (I.C.I.). Finally, in 1884, in conjunction with Hazart and Cosgen, the Solvay Process Company (United States) built the first American factory in Syracuse and some time later, another plant in Detroit.

In 1888, at the time of the company's 25th anniversary, an extensive network of soda works was in place in all the main industrialized countries and overall annual production reached 350000 tons. This was only the beginning since the present production figures are in the region of 4 million tons annually.

In addition, and despite the fact that soda production was given prime importance, a range of by-products and other sectors were developed — such as pure bicarbonate of soda, soda cristals, caustic soda and salts, table salt and hydrochloric acid. Production units for potash, which is similar to soda, were built at Roschwitz and phosphate mines were worked at Mons and in the Somme region, the young companies being financed by older well-established ones. At that time, caustic soda was the main application for carbonate and was produced using a causticizing process based mainly on a liming process. This was easily incorporated into the production techniques for soda, since this produced lime and steam from the carbonate. Solvay set up his network of causticizing activities in parallel with the soda works which used large quantities of carbonate; this was before the introduction, in 1898, of electrolysis which revolutionized this industry.

The intervening period between the company's 10th and 25th anniversaries was to be fertile in important decisions and achievements. It was during these years that the Solvay group really came into being and that Ernest Solvay developed the company's work ethic, its special way of doing business and finally its social charter which the adjustments to today's attitudes have

not altered in any way.

    At the same time, he received many honors. He was award-
ed a modest bronze medal at the 1867 World Exhibition held in
Paris. In 1873, Vienna presented him with an honorary degree
and in 1878 Philadephia honored him with the First Prize. These
many high honors probably did not mean as much to him as his
very first award, received at the age of 20, of 2000 francs together
with the congratulations from the Board of Directors of his uncle's gas plant in Saint-Josse, on the apparatus he had developed
to prevent obstruction of the gas pipes. In addition, this encouragement probably acted as further stimulus and put him on the road
to fame; for, only a short while later, while looking for new outlets
for the ammonia recovered in coal distillation, he discovered the

*Dombasle, (France),
historically the
Group's second
plant, constructed
in 1872 on the site
of a large salt
deposit.*

54

main chemical reaction underlying the production method for soda based on ammonia. His genius for invention together with his obstination were to lead him, from then on, to his numerous very well-documented successes.

At the time of the celebrations held on November 17, 1888 for the Solvays' 25 years at the head of the company, Ernest Solvay made a speech demonstrating his lucidity of mind and prescience: «Industries, like man, grow old and after 25 years of marriage we very often only celebrate the ravages of time... This must not befall us... but how is this to be avoided? Quite simply, by uniting more firmly that which already exists in all the various countries, by extending this unity to a wider circle of operations and by improving the guidelines and rules that each factory has developed and implemented; by maintaining and strengthening the governing principles concerning work and action... in one word, by creating such an intimate, powerful and wide-reaching alliance that it presents only the advantages of a multinational company and none of the disadvantages and difficulties. It is thanks to the collaboration of a great many alumni directing their attention to a certain number of goals that one may reduce, for a fairly long time, the financial risks inherent in our business activities. This is the only way in which it is possible to ensure stability and longevity and also the industry's enduring youthfulness.»

This man whose vision reached beyond the limits of a region, of a country, of even a continent, went on to state (over a century ago, let us not forget) what seem to be Europe's present beliefs at a time of change and new opportunities: «I have the conviction that the future belongs to those who invest in wide-reaching collaboration and common interests. This is the price that must be paid. Ever since we marked out these new goals, we are constantly being presented with justification of our choice of strategy. Our industrial environment seems to be changing. But what a difference there is between the emerging financial connections, the vast complexes with no central planning, no unity and these very powerful synergies of work and intelligence, tempered by many years of application and which we merely wish to make perfect.»

*From the outset, the
Solvay brothers
understood the
importance that
their production
method would have
throughout the
world...*

56

Some of the company's geographical milestones.

IV. CONFIRMATION

The British soda makers basing their production on Leblanc's process were growing increasingly worried. Ernest Solvay had foreseen the development of his process which even today is still regarded as the best. The patents taken out in 1863, 1872 and 1876 contained all the essential improvements which their practical application made increasingly evident.

It is possible that they considered Ernest Solvay to be of similar scientific ability as Dyar and Hemming or Schloesing and Rolland, when in fact they were dealing with an industrialist determined to succeed. Up to then, soda made from ammonia had only been a laboratory success story and had not been applicable on an industrial level. However, Ernest Solvay, was to take this process one step further and he may thus justifiably be considered as the industry's founding father.

Solvay knew that as far as industry was concerned, there was no middle road between eternal youthfulness and obsolescence.

One of the company's rejuvenating elements was the discovery of mercury electrolysis which he launched in 1898 at Jemeppe-sur-Sambre, Belgium. The basic principles of electrolysis had been established since the middle of the 19th century, since tests using electric currents had already been carried out. In 1891, a chemical plant in Frankfurt-am-Main, Germany, produced caustic potash using electrolysis. Subsequently, it also produced caustic soda and chlorine using this same technique. The Solvays had taken note of this development and were well aware that the use of electrolysis would ensure their victory over the Leblanc soda workers, who were skeptical of this because of the limited uses for chlorine which was a by-product of electrolysis. Ernest Solvay had repeatedly reiterated his 1886 statement to the company's Supervisory Board and was to do so again on December 1, 1893, stating: «I need chlorine... our production process will, like all others, become obsolete, losing its leading role.»

It was a man of such pessimism who presided over the company's fate at a time of major expansion. The long-term plans together with investments in France, Austria, Russia and America had drained a substantial amount of the company's financial means.

*Machine room at
the Jemeppe plant.*

The company was to have a controlling interest in its mineral resources and the German Management Team encouraged plans for drilling operations which would mean that the company would own the very large potash deposits. Alfred and Ernest Solvay were undecided, hesitant to launch this project since this industry's costs did not concern them as much as those of the soda industry. They were finally persuaded to go ahead and did not regret their decision. They had always been extremely interested in all forms of mineral deposits.

Electrolysis was to open the way to success. Having taken out German patents, they bought up an English test site and developed their own electrolysis cells using mercury cathodes. They therefore finally obtained the chlorine which they had previously lacked, together with caustic soda which they did not produce in large quantities. Their first electrolysis plant was inaugurated in 1898 at Jemeppe-sur-Sambre, 20kms from Couillet.

They were set to dominate both sectors and their leading position would never come under attack, since they relied on the cheapest sources of carbonate and could choose between caustic soda production based either on electrolysis or on causticizing. In the long term, electrolysis gained sufficient ground leading to the obsolescence of the causticizing procedure.

The company made strides and nothing would stop its progress. Its first factory was launched at Couillet in the Charleroi region and the subsequent factories were to have the following names: Dombasle, Northwich, Sandbach, Middlewich, Lostock, Berezniki, Donetz, Syracuse, Detroit, Sarralbe, Château-Salins, Wyhlen, Rheinberg, Würselen, Bernburg, Ebensee, Nestomitz, Lukavac, Maros-Ujvar, Lieres, Polanco, Torrelavega, Rosignano and were built in various regions of France, Great Britain, Russia, United States, Alsace-Lorraine, Germany, the Austro-Hungarian Empire, Spain and Italy. The Solvay name reigned supreme and the factories were busy extracting, converting, producing and also provided many people with jobs. On the eve of World War I, i.e. at the time of the company's 50th anniversary, production of carbonate of soda, using the method which had made the Leblanc process obsolete, had reached a staggering 2 million tons — 90% of world production and the company owned 24 factories worldwide.

We shall have the opportunity of discussing Solvay's subsequent development in the last chapters of this book. For now, we would like to touch on another aspect of the man who had

*Below:
electrolysis plant
at Jemeppe-sur-
Sambre, Belgium.*

said «I can not help but pity those who look to the past, who endeavor to maintain the status quo, who find their negativism in sleepiness, narrow-mindedness, in the selfishness of the privileged or in their fear of what is new and use this as a defense to counter just demands. Tomorrow's world must either be governed by justice or disappear.»

*Photo on following
pages: electrolysis
room at Jemeppe.*

SOCIAL CONSIDERATIONS

I. ERNEST SOLVAY AND HIS PLAN

It is most unusual to find scientists who are also inventors and industrialists and it is even rarer when they are innovators in social matters. Ernest Solvay was that man. It may have come as a result of having had to give up his studies, spending hours reading and pondering alone in his room instead of in university lecture halls like other students of his age. It is true that self-taught people are not the only ones to have a soft heart. Yet they are rarely called upon at an age at which their fellow-students have not yet left university, to manage a company and to see at close hand the workers' living and working conditions.

Ernest Solvay had this opportunity and wrote down his feelings, becoming deeply involved throughout his long life and combined these driving forces, i.e. thought, social action and industrial activity. Is it really possible to understand such a person fully? His private life is not very well known: he married his young cousin, Adèle Winderickx in 1863, just two months before the constitution of his company, Solvay & Cie. They had two sons and two daughters, Armand and Edmond, Jeanne and Hélène. Ernest Sougnez wrote in his book «Souvenirs de famille» (published in Brussels in 1935) that «*his wife lived in admiration of her husband and was throughout the many years of very happy married life his understanding and supportive companion... close collaboration and constant and discrete assistance. Such self-effacing roles are difficult to evaluate and thus the more valuable. To understand is to be someone's equal.*» His family tree included such well-known families as the Janssens, the Selliers de Moranvilles, the Boëls, the Hankars, the Nieuwenhuys', the Gendebiens, the Rolins, the't Kint de Roodenbekes, the de la Barre d'Erquelinnes', the Washers.. The following families are all his brothers' and sisters' descendants and also those of the company's original investors: the Semets, the Aubertins, the Delwarts, the Ganshof van der Merschs, the Wangens, the Laguiches, the Bautiers, the Quertons, the Dorlodots, the Crawhez' and the Pirmez'. About 4000 people make up these family descendants and are still present today at the Stockholders' Meeting and on the company's Board of Directors. They are representative of Belgian society, being active in industry and are to be seen in the capital's fashionable circles. Ernest was succeeded by Armand, his eldest son, by Louis, Alfred's son, by Ernest-John, Ernest's grandson and Jacques, his great-grandson. All his descendants, like René Boël, Ernest's granddaughter's husband and at present Daniel Janssen, a fifth generation descendant have always taken great pains to follow the company's tradition of laying more value on merit than on family connexions, on equal chances and group unity and finally pragmatism together with enlightened vision.

Ernest was neither a great lover of the Arts, nor able to practice sports due to poor health, although as a child he had enjoyed athletics and wrestling and played the local ball game of « balle pelote ». He had to wait a long time before recovering sufficient fitness to be able to go mountaineering. He was 57 years old and from that age on, he would enjoy his new-found hobby every summer, still climbing Swiss peaks at the age of 81. To help meditation, he would walk every day in the Bois de la Cambre and the Forêt de Soignes, on the outskirts of Brussels. Many times and right up to his death, he could be seen walking the 17 kms from his residence in La Hulpe, to his office in Ixelles and every morning he would do some limbering exercises, saying that they were good for his health.

If as the saying goes, the early bird catches the worm, then Ernest Solvay was certain to be successful and to achieve what he had set out to do. He was up every morning at 5 am and went early to bed, at around 10 pm. He apparently had a ferocious appetite at lunchtime but drunk only a little wine or beer and did not smoke.

Two photographs, taken at an interval of 60 years, show a young man of certain charm and an old man of great distinction. The first one was to revolutionize industry entirely and the second was to have an enormous influence on society. Although it was not until 1894 that he set up the Institute for Social Sciences in the Hôtel Ravenstein, in Brussels, he had already been pondering things for some time. For him, wealth was only a means and not an end in itself and he would later put his money and name at the disposal of society through the promotion of charitable institutions and Science in general. One important event to prove this point was the allocation of the company's first dividend to the personnel's charity fund.

You will remember that the first soda works was built in 1863 at Couillet, near Charleroi. In 1868, roving bands of local mineworkers carried out acts of vandalism at the Epine mine at Dampremy and were repelled by the troops which had been called in. The shooting left ten dead, including 2 women and led to many being injured. Ernest Solvay was greatly shocked by this particular incident and also the events of the 1871 Paris Commune, leading him to write an article which he signed «*A Thinker*» and which was published in the Brussels newspaper «*L'Office de Publicité*». In this article, he insisted on the necessity of providing schooling for a larger number and of evolving a social code based on the well-known but little practiced saying: *do to others as you would have them do to you*.

A few years later in 1879, at the age of only 41, he published

Ernest Solvay mountaineering.

a brochure called «*Science and Religion, from a social viewpoint*», from which it may be useful to cite some passages.

The author starts from the following premise: in Belgium, after Independence, liberal catholicism was followed in 1875 by a wave of intolerance and fanaticism against lay principles which were the basis of modern society. *Science* (which was, according to Ernest Solvay, *the philosophy issuing from the natural sciences*) was freeing society from orthodox catholic values. He analyzed the main discoveries made in geology, physics, chemistry and astronomy and touched on sociology, declaring that human conscience was shaped gradually by scientific discoveries. Freedom of choice does not exist.

He went on to say: «We are completely dominated by the laws of nature, each of our thoughts has a cause and this in turn also has a cause, so that we can go back in time to the original cause, i.e. the origins of thought. Human freedom is therefore a myth and humanity, as a whole, is propelled (with plant life) into the future where at the end of time, we discover the infallible and overpowering laws of progress and evolution. We have lived through a very long period of virtual intellectual and moral stagnation while at the same time, enormous material development has been achieved... A very long list of demands has been made and even their temporary suppression cannot entirely kill the seeds of discontent. On the contrary, they have been given life since they have been fought for with arms and not with the truth, i.e. science. A *practical, social* ethic must be justified and its only foundation must be justice.»

Ernest Solvay in his generosity did not accept that some had a more difficult start in life, one that he would not have wanted himself. Conditions must be equal for all. Having accepted the fact that we come into this life as either aristocrats or commoners, masters or valets, rich or poor, he petitioned for the riddance of these inequalities, stating «for an association of intelligent beings to be what it claims to be, that is a society offering the same advantages and opportunities for all. None must be resentful of their start in life». The moment has come to think about the future of our society. Social conditions must be improved if we are to avoid a terrible upheaval. This can be achieved by the application of a single tax, a form of «*primogenitus*» obligation in favor of the State, and the gradual disappearance of all hereditary social inequalities which can be equated with slavery and the original oppression of the under-privileged.

Ernest Solvay had stated two of his main ideas, *an equal start in life* and a *single tax on inherited wealth*. He was to develop these ideas in what he called «*Productivisme*» and «*Comptabilisme*». These two theories are very interesting but somewhat specialized to be dealt with here at length. Ernest Solvay was not a man out of touch with reality, nor had the many years spent in a laboratory hardened his feelings. He had observed and been shocked by the terrible scenes of misery. Yet many of the young nation's leaders seemed less concerned than he by the revolt which was growing and which had its roots in the working classes' abject conditions. After 20 years of Independence, Frère-Orban painted an idyllic picture of Belgian society. Thirty-five years later and despite the 1886 national crisis, the riots, fires and the many dead, Auguste Beernaert said in the Chamber of Representatives: «Our social organization, although not perfect, is constantly being improved. Crises erupt but they are only temporary... The overriding rule we have noted is that interest rates are on the decrease and very soon there will be no capitalist who can afford to live without working. At the same time, the workload is increasing and we must, therefore, not intervene; a free market must be left to flourish».

He did not appear to realize that the worker was not encouraged to produce more. His meagre salary meant that he had little to eat and therefore lacked the energy to work better and harder. He had little education and did not always understand how best to carry out his work.

What did Solvay notice?

— that where there was a pay structure based on piece work, the worker was encouraged to produce more. However, the employer would then reduce the promised unit rate;

— that production often outstripped demand, making for disorganization, which led to economic recession and unemployment;

— that business was badly organized and the scene of much fraud, such as falsification of products and their net weights or profits in excess of the finished products' value;

— that finance and its attending fraud, mismanagement, speculation and deceit were ruining the working classes and creating a very volatile social climate.

This is what an informed person would have made of the situation which was much less attractive than politicians had previously depicted.

They ought to have been much more aware of national discontent and of the fact that the working classes were beginning to organize themselves, demanding a say in the running of the country and the suppression of the social injustices to which they were subjected.

The «Parti Ouvrier» (Labor Party) was formed and, in 1894, plural voting was introduced. Although this was a step towards equality, it nevertheless favored the privileged and the rural classes.

This same year, Solvay founded the Institute for Social Sciences and called upon Hector Denis, Guillaume De Greef and Emile Vandervelde to manage this new institution. His social charter was the result of his observations concerning the social situation which needed to be remedied by replacing industrial anarchy with order and wage injustices with an equitable structure. The improvements would be of great benefit to the producers as well as to the consumers.

What were the guidelines of this well-intentioned social charter? Ever-increasing production in order to develop public welfare. According to Ernest Solvay, the guiding theory behind social development is productivism, but this is also accompanied by other factors mentioned below:

— what he called in French «comptabilisme» which allows for the circulation of a larger quantity of capital funds by abolishing hard currency and monetary interest, by organizing financial transactions and by reducing trade discounts to a minimum;

— the principle of an equal start in life which is a means of creating a greater number of efficient and intelligent work units;

— «unemployment linked to further education» which will be sustained by the development of primary and technical education in order to achieve this same result;

— the assurance of wealth, free collectivization together with an interest in industrial and commercial activities whose aim is to reduce capital waste, to eradicate fraud and financial mismanagement and to ensure progressive collectivization should the general public so demand;

— single taxation on death which is nothing other than the protection of incipient wealth, i.e. production and therefore the abolition of parasitic behavior, capital waste by ineffectual, wasteful and lazy members of society.

Solvay thought that the application of such a productivist social system would, in the long term, lead to the disappearance, on a national level, of individual economic anarchy. If this social system were to be applied universally, State economic anarchy would also be abolished. Are we not on the right path towards this objective when occasionally one may notice a momentary and unexpected flash of international harmony? Solvay thought so, adding «If this international harmony included all nations irrespectively and if these participated in the deliberations and decisions (not because of their military might — which is absurd, belonging to barbaric times), but in proportion to their production (which is only equitable, logical and profitable to efficient and active nations whose contributions can easily be worked out when international «comptabilisme» has been established), an enormous step forward will have been taken towards the goals to be reached, i.e. peace and a universal society».

One may dream! One may talk of utopia! Others before him had worked out social reforms which he strenuously denied having copied, claiming he had not the time to study these and that he wished to keep his intellectual and investigative independence. He felt concerned only by general considerations and facts.

Thirteen years before Ernest Solvay's birth, Count Henri de Saint-Simon died. Born into a wealthy family and having earned great sums of money, he died in poverty, leaving his friends 100000 francs for the development of the Sciences and general instruction, which was to be a forerunner to the Institut Solvay. After having fought under Washington during the American War of Independence, he left the army to become involved in social reforms. In 1844, he published a pamphlet entitled *Réorganisation de la société européenne* (The Reorganization of European Society), in which he called for a Greater European Parliament to be established. In his *Système industriel* (industrial system), he demanded the abolition, without exception, of all inherited privileges, the emancipation of the workers, the suppression of idleness, honor, wealth and respect for and of industrialists, scholars and artists, the gradual suppression of farm rents, universal collaboration in favor of peace, the suppression of transferred inheritance laws (to the State).

Mention should be made of some other French social reformers, such as Louis Blanc and P.-J. Proudhon. The former fought the practice of free trade which penalized the weaker members of society. He wished to replace this with an organizational structure, based on everyone's right to work and placed under the aegis of the State which would open workshops. The

latter favored barter based on work vouchers which would lead to the abolition of money as such, and therefore also of interest in money.

Their contemporary, François Vidal, defended the idea of a bank which would not be based on money. It would collect payment for sold products and would pay the money-orders for all the various supplies made out by merchants, industrialists and producers with current or deposit account at the bank. Since the institution would collect and pay on behalf of all its clients, cash books, bank payments and bank transfers would render bank notes obsolete.

To conclude this rapid survey of early and middle 19th century social reformers, one must mention the Welshman Robert Owen, a self-confessed Communist. He declared that consumer and producer cooperatives would keep capital and employment in the same hands and that therefore, exchange practices and the use of money would also have to be reformed.

Saint-Simon was the founder of the school named after him and had considerable influence during the first half of the 19th century.

Solvay's five predecessors all showed the same preoccupations and were all imbued with a desire to work for mankind's happiness. However, none had drawn up plans that were as wide-ranging and as pragmatic as his and which could constitute the basis of a government bill. They were men of ideas but Solvay was a man of action for whom increased welfare was linked to a better distribution of the purveyors' consumer goods.

He was not interested in politics. However, when the constitution was to be revised in 1893, he was prevailed upon by his friend, Paul Janson, to be one of the Liberal Party's election candidates, since he wished to have a very public forum to defend his ideas. He was elected as Senator for Brussels and accepted a new mandate in 1897 which he occupied until 1900. A man of such vision must have suffered under the narrow-mindedness of the opinions expressed on matters concerning the present, saying on December 27, 1899: «Gentlemen, while the Senate is busy with matters concerning the present... I myself am more especially concerned with the future...» and again on March 22, 1900: «To be sure, I have already taken the liberty of remarking upon this fact that if all the questions of day-to-day concern with which the Senate is confronted are of utmost interest, I myself find it impossible to believe that there are no other new

*Four generations:
Ernest Solvay,
1838;
Armand Solvay,
1865;
Ernest-John Solvay,
1895;
Jacques Solvay,
1920.*

77

and long-term views which ought to retain the Senate's attention».
In his speech of December 1899, he expressed his wish to see
the State become the main participant in all the nation's activities.
Citizens would be invited to entrust the State, instead of the banks,
with their money. The more they gave it, the more it would invest
in other concerns. Private enterprise and initiative which is the
source of all business would in no way suffer but the State would
increasingly collectivize, aided and abetted by the circumstances.
Ernest Solvay had imagined a theoretical collective state based
on the fact that all enterprise would have been collectivized by
continued application of the basic principle of freedom. He maintained that private initiative would always be respected and that
it would, in the last resort, only exist to provide workers with
substantially higher wages, equivalent to a salary in industry or
business rather than in the civil service.

In Ernest Solvay's State, justice for all would reign supreme
and production would be protected. This, however, did not take
the powers of inertia, routine and vested interests into consideration. Such a form of «socialism» had not the slightest chance of
succeeding other than maybe within the framework of a company
and so the two brothers were to be the front-runners in adopting
the above-mentioned social principles. Their enemies could well
claim that their social charter was only inspired by the wish to
avoid social conflict which would have been very surprising
behavior in two very generous and compassionate human beings. Only their achievements really count and these were greatly in advance of the times!

THE SOCIAL PLAN

1. *An equal start in life*. - Laws protecting early infancy, leading to the setting-up in all boroughs of state-funded canteens for expectant and nursing mothers, baby clinics and free milk distribution. The obligation to attend school and generalization of 4th year vocational training classes. Periodic visits by the students to factories and workshops to be able to choose their future profession with appropriate judgment. Mandatory vocational and technical training for girls and boys. School meals for all, thanks to Government funds.

2. *The right to life*. - Laws ensuring sickness benefits in the event of illness, accident, disablement and old age; public welfare reforms, joint or regional insurance for involuntary unemployment and benefit payments by the boroughs, provinces and the State.

3. *The Labor market*. - Setting-up of labor exchanges to provide work for the unemployed and vocational training for young people out of work («chomage-capacitariat»).

4. *Productivisme* (Productivism). - Free socialization. Review of the law on commercial companies, the objective being to protect savings and to interest the State in the creation either of new companies and corporations or in the capital increase of existing companies.

5. *General Savings Bank*. - Reorganization in order to collect as many funds as possible, enabling the State to take part in the creation or the development of industrial, commercial or agricultural companies and possibly even to participate, at borough and inter-borough levels, in certain public services of common interest.

6. *Comptabilisme*. - Reorganization of the National Bank through the creation of agencies or branch offices in all the production centers, provision of credit at cost price, direct credit to credit unions as well as to agricultural, consumer and producer cooperatives, by the setting-up of a «comptabilist» office, with the assistance of post offices, working in parallel with the present transfer and exchange system.

7. *New funds to be created*. - Estate duties.

II. THE ACHIEVEMENTS

At the end of the last century, Ernest and Alfred Solvay adopted an 8-hour working day and by 1907, this was to be general policy throughout their company. This was later legalized in 1921 throughout Belgium.

Sickness benefits, which became mandatory in 1945, were already general practice at Solvay by 1878. Pensions and double holiday money were also introduced for all their employees in 1913 although paid holidays only became official in 1936 and initially was only equal to one month's salary. Double holiday money was introduced later in 1948. Starting in 1890, they organized consumer cooperatives, independent companies managed by their employees and workers and providing services and loans. Their social charter, submitted 4 years later to the Senate, listed consumer goods in the following order of importance: food, clothing, housing, protection, education and leisure.

What was done to improve food supplies? Stores were set up in those areas where supplies were badly organized in order to provide the company's personnel with food at reasonable prices. Arable land, which was tilled and manured at the company's expense, was rented out to the workers at very low cost to help them supplement their meagre household income.

Clothing was provided by women's sewing groups who were also helped in this endeavor by the setting-up of sewing classes. Sewing machines were also rented out and to help with housing, a loans' system was launched in 1892.

Two years earlier, the company inaugurated its first hospital which included laboratories and operating theaters and also a nursing home which was the fore runner to the very official home nursing system which came into existence only much later.

In 1881, the Solvay brothers launched the setting-up of libraries, training colleges for professional instruction and adult education classes which were held in the factories. Instruction for children was provided in purpose-built schools, together with grants for the best among them. Technical training colleges made their appearance in the workers' housing estates.

The Solvays also paid attention to their personnel's leisure time activities and since they were from Belgium's «balle pelote» playing region, they of course provided support for this game.

They also financed the creation of a local fanfare at Jemeppe-sur-Sambre, rifle clubs and gymnastic teams and subsequently provided liberally for all forms of sport. This policy was applied to all the Group's factories at home and abroad. The word «social» was never without meaning, neither for their descendants nor for their successors. It should also be stated that Ernest Solvay provided substantial financial support for a long list of Universities such as those in Brussels, Nancy, Paris, Geneva and Charleroi. He also helped researchers and scientists (such as Marie Curie) whose research work was seriously jeopardized due to monetary problems. He also commissioned Baron Horta, the famous Belgian architect, to build several town houses in Brussels and also a memorial to his brother Alfred in Couillet.

A worker's housing estate and hospital were generally built in the vicinity of the Solvay plants...

...a school, a sports
and community
center.

83

III. THE INSTITUTIONS

Although hard work had fostered success, it was seriously to undermine Ernest's health and lead to Alfred's death. Ernest Solvay was the first to consult his doctor, Dr. Paul Héger who told him in no uncertain terms that he should submit to medical attention. He agreed and left for Carlsbad, from which he returned in 1884 after a long stay during which he had taken a liking to solitude and long walks which restored his health and which would help him to enjoy a long life.

On his return, he wrote to Paul Héger, starting a long exchange of letters based on the two men's great interest in science. In 1888, Solvay informed his friend of his intention of setting up a research laboratory to confirm or refute his personal scientific views. The following year, the electro-physics laboratory was established in rue des Sols in Brussels. This laboratory was to be so successful that it had to be further expanded. Dr. Héger mentioned the Parc Léopold as a possibility and Solvay submitted his project to the town authorities.

On June 18, 1892 an agreement was signed between Ernest Solvay and Mayor Buls, the Mayor of Brussels, concerning Solvay's wish to develop, on the one hand, research begun in 1889 together with other scientific research, and on the other hand, to help the Brussels' central authorities endow its university with the necessary institutes and laboratories for applied scientific studies. The town's central authorities would subsequently provide Ernest Solvay with a site of about 360 square meters in the Parc Léopold for the construction of the University Institute of Physiology and a second site of about 950 square meters for a scientific school

From left to right: The Solvay Institutes for Physiology, Business Studies and Sociology, as seen in a picture published in the «Le Temps» newspaper's illustrated supplement, September 1920.

to be named after Ernest Solvay.

In exchange, the first building would, on inauguration, become the property of Brussels' central authorities, the second building also to become its property on expiry or termination of the signed 30-year agreement. In addition, E. Solvay would remit a sum of 10000 francs to the town's central authorities for the conversion or construction of a) housing for the Park's wardens, b) an orangery and c) a toolshed. He would also agree to provide 200000 francs (gold, of course) for the construction and furnishing of the University Institute, together with additional scientific equipment for its laboratories. The same amount at least was to be provided for the Institut Solvay.

He also agreed, for the duration of the convention, to bear the full costs arising out of all necessary repairs, reconstruction and renewal of his institute and would also pay all taxes and expenses. It was therefore not surprising that the Brussels' City Fathers agreed unanimously upon the submitted project and convention. On May 19, 1892, they betook themselves in person to the donor's residence to thank him on behalf of the town's central authorities and presented him with a commemorative medal which had been created by the sculptor Fernand Dubois. The future mayor of Brussels, Emile De Mot, was a member of the delegation.

Only three examples of this special medal had been made, one in gold, one in silver (probably intended for the District Museum) and a third one in bronze which was sealed into the Institute's foundations. On the coin's obverse side, one can see the donor's profile and the inscription: «*La Ville de Bruxelles reconnaissante à Ernest Solvay*» (The Town of Brussels grateful to Ernest Solvay). The reverse side shows an allegoric figure representing Science, with the inscription: «*Omnia in mensura*» and below «*Fondation des Instituts universitaires, 4 juillet 1892*» (Foundation of the University Institutes, July 4, 1892).

Construction of the new institute began on that date. It was finished so quickly, under Dr Paul Héger's supervision, that the University Institute of Physiology was able to give theoretical and practical lectures in the 1893 October term. The «electro-biological» research laboratories were inaugurated two months later. Ernest Solvay published a speech on «The Role of Electricity in the Phenomena of Life» in which he started from the premise that «the phenomena of Life can and must be explained through the interplay of the universe's physical forces and that among these forces, electricity plays a major role». He considered the tissues requiring major oxydation (and more especially the muscles) as being a generating apparatus, the nerves as conductors and the nerve centers as switchboards and not as energy-generating. For him, Life was characterized not so much by special morphological conditions but more by the existence of an organized system of continuous reactions in which the elements were constantly being regenerated. To conclude, he stated that «he was expecting the very rigorous experimenting, carried out in the widest possible manner, to provide an impartial and in-depth study of the system which had for a long time occupied his thoughts.»

*

* *

Ernest Solvay had many scientific preoccupations. Was he not to concede in a speech in 1893: «I do not have the great fortune to be a man of Science. I did not receive much in the way of traditional education. Industrial problems have taken up all my time and thoughts but it is true that I have pursued a scientific goal because I like Science because I expect it to provide progress for all humanity.» He began by striving to reduce the phenomenon of Life to physical and chemical laws. He subsequently had the conviction that based on purely scientific considerations, he might be able to study the social phenomena, and that each human group, and thus mankind generally, developed according to certain laws. Starting out from physical energy, he followed on with psychological energy, finally to end with social energy.

His train of thought had its roots in late 19th century scientific thought. However, he did not content himself with just observing the social situation of his times. He strove for progressive, continuous and indefinite improvement in mankind's welfare through the optimization of human energy. An improvement in the worker's lot and peace in the workplace would only be achieved through gradual modification of the social situation. In 1894 he wrote the following to the Senate: «*Economic and intellectual progress must be accelerated because if we do not encourage this, conditions will force us beyond what is reasonable and practical, leading to violence and tragic human conditions.*» Such insight is not often seen in the business or political world: it is true that Ernest Solvay came to politics by accident and did not consider his assistants as machines.

The Physics Institute was set up by the scientific community to confirm or refute Solvay's physics theories, the Sociology In-

The Solvay Physics Council, Brussels 1911. Seated from left to right: Nernst, Brillouin, Solvay, Lorentz, Warburg, Perrin, Wien, Mme Curie, Poincaré.

Standing from left to right: Goldschmidt, Planck, Rubens, Sommerfeld, Lindemann, de Broglie, Knudsen, Hasenohrl, Hostelet, Herzen, Jeans, Rutherford, Kamerlingh Onnes, Einstein, Langevin.

stitute would likewise group specialists to verify his social theories. This institution had a dual connexion with the Physiology Institute. On the one hand, it was based on the same scientific rigor on which Solvay had insisted in the demonstration of his personal convictions and on the other hand, on the necessary link he had created between the social sciences and biology.

Solvay also set up the Institute for Social Sciences which was housed, further to an agreement reached with the District authorities, in one of the rooms of the Hôtel Ravenstein in Brussels and where the League of Women's Rights and the League against Alcoholism were also to be found.

Solvay entrusted three socialists close to his own social convictions with the initial research into the theory of «comptabilisme»: Emile Vandervelde, Hector Denis and Guillaume De Greef. The first was a well-known political figure right up to his death; the second had already opened a psycho-physical laboratory at Brussels University and the third had developed a theory which was very similar to Solvay's, evaluating the biological means necessary to appreciate the sociological means. Ernest Solvay provided them with 15000 francs annually for three years, 12000 of which was a personal grant.

However, the days of this Institute of Social Sciences were up and it was replaced by the Institute of Sociology. Solvay had met Emile Waxweiler, a sociologist with a degree from the Engineering Institute in Ghent. He was a member of the International Institute of Statistics, a civil servant with the Ministry of Industry and Employment and professor at the Université Libre de Bruxelles (U.L.B.). E. Waxweiler, L. Wodon and G. Demarez (both professors at Brussels University) were to work with Ernest Solvay who was preparing the draft statutes which, while defining the institute's research areas (especially financial questions), also defined its far-reaching aims: «The Institute's purpose is the scientific study of all facets of social phenomena. It is to carry this out mainly from the theoretical point of view of progress made in the social sciences as well as from the practical point of view of social reforms and research into those problems mentioned by its founder in his *notes on «comptabilisme» and «productivisme»*. Did he foresee gaps in his social plan?

This draft project was not signed by Ernest Solvay himself since he wished to be given prior assurance from the town's central authorities. On February 12, 1901, he sent the authorities the following letter in which one may read:

«... Economic and social problems are paramount in our present-day social preoccupations; these last few years have seen a great increase in the studies and research carried out in this field... In order to be able to continue these studies to which I have applied myself and to provide all researchers with the means to contribute to the progress in social sciences, I intend to set up an Institute of Sociology in Brussels.

The Institute's buildings should, to my mind, include a fully-equipped library, a series of study rooms, accessible to all men of Science wishful of undertaking research into sociology and also a lecture hall.

On the other hand, since I wish to include higher education in the movement of the mind towards observation and the positive study of social phenomena, I propose to provide for the future of the School of Political and Social Sciences which is part of Brussels University...

This joint foundation would enable greater application of investigative and teaching methods to the social sciences, these methods having already provided brilliant results in the fields of physico-chemistry and biology.

The City Fathers have already kindly put at my disposal a site in the Parc Léopold where the Institute of Physiology is now located. I should indeed be very happy, should I be able to build on this same site a new Institute which would thus finalize the small «scientific site» which the honorable Mr Buls wished to see created and to which he referred in his report to the Town Council on June 27, 1892.

I believe a maximum of 1350 square meters to be enough for the realization of my project and in the event that the City Fathers agree to grant me, for a duration of 25 years, a neighboring site, I would agree, upon expiry of this period, to hand over the new Institute's buildings together with its furnishings and scientific equipment. It is agreed that I shall bear all costs for repairs, taxes and contributions, etc... similar to those fixed by the 1892 agreement... for the duration of the above-mentioned period.»

It is obviously not necessary to mention the authorities' response to this proposal; it was of course positive. However, four months elapsed before official notification of the approval was given.

On June 4, 1901, Ernest Solvay had let his assistants know that he had believed it necessary to make some alterations to his original project in order to consolidate the institute's legal situation and discharge his assistants of all administrative work. He appointed a single director, Emile Waxweiler, to be his representative. The original project provided for the Institute's management to be renewed by co-opting the other members, i.e. Emile Vandervelde, Hector Denis and Guillaume De Greef. They protested, saying that they were only considered as scientific colleagues. Solvay's refusal to discuss the matter with them and their refusal to discuss with anyone else led to a rift and finally to separation. Solvay made each of them a generous gift of 11000 francs in consideration of their collaboration.

This conflict can only be explained by a difference in ideology. The trio's collectivist ideas were not adaptable to the industrialist's reformist views. He was a man who made ideas fit the facts and not the facts fit ideas. He explained his viewpoint in letters to Edouard Anseele, socialist Representative, to whom he felt very

First Solvay Chemistry Council, Brussels 1922.
First row:
Moureu, Aston, Bragg, Armstrong, Pope, Solvay, Haller, Arrhénius and Soddy.
Second row:
Delépine, Biilmann, Wuyts, Lowry, Urbain, Perrin, Jaeger, Debierne, Rupe, Berthoud and Pickard.
Third row:
Chavanne, Dony-Hénault, Swarts, Mauguin, Herzen, Flamache, Hannon and Piccard.

close and to the Senate where he was not thought to be a right-of-center liberal. It was neither his aim nor his intention to be considered as the protector of the Socialist Party. He wrote to Anseele, saying: «...*maybe you have only to break away from the local notion of social progress in order to adopt a more universal concept...*» He declared to the Assembly: «At the Institute, I am surrounded by men who are naturally of good disposition but who nevertheless are influenced, like others, by present-day doctrines from which they must first break away...»

Towards the end of June 1901, the Institute's statutes were finalized and E. Waxweiler, L. Wodon and G. Desmarez were in charge of the day-to-day management; on June 4, Waxweiler already had 21000 francs at his disposal for the initial expenses. The annual grant was subsequently increased to 50000 francs (gold) annually for the duration of the agreement with the Town

Council, which meant that the last and final payment had to be made by January 1, 1926. E. Solvay provided further funds: in 1909 and 1910, for instance, he gave 75000 francs towards the Institute's 3-year experimental organization of an international sociology information office.

In theory, there was no link between the Université Libre de Bruxelles and the Institute since the latter was the property of E. Solvay for a period of 25 years. In fact, there was a connexion, the first being the free thinking which governed all the studies at both institutions. E. Solvay had also involved his foundation in the development of the «Social School», where E. Waxweiler was a professor. Finally, one year after the creation of the Institute of Sociology, the Université Libre de Bruxelles (U.L.B.) opened a Business School (Ecole de Commerce) which was not only named after Solvay but also subsidized by him and directed by Waxweiler. This new school was also located in the Parc Léopold where it was to remain for half a century before joining the University at Solbosch (a district of Brussels).

Léopold II, who was also a businessman, had expressed his wish to the University's Board of Governors concerning the setting-up, in the capital, of a School of Business Studies. This was on June 3, 1903 and on June 3 of the following year, E. Solvay announced his plans to the administrators-inspectors of the U.L.B. of fulfilling the royal wish: «... I have thus come to ask you whether you would agree to develop classes along these lines (truly comprehensive course of university-level commercial studies) and organize the creation of a School of Political and Social Sciences.» Let us not forget that he helped to instill very advanced economics teaching in this school and which the Institute of Sociology's training further enhanced. He agreed to bear the running costs for this Business and Management Faculty of the Institute for a period of ten years. In the event that the experiment was deemed successful, he would renew his gesture for a further ten years.

Having obtained the District authorities' approval, he built the Business School between the Physiology and Sociology Institutes. It was considered as an annex to the Political and Social Sciences Faculties. E. Solvay requested that its teaching not be exclusively professional.

Since this Business School had its own funds on which its existence and longevity depended, it was considered as an annex to the U.L.B. Its management was under the supervision of the U.L.B. but it nevertheless had its own separate organization, administration and budget and its faculty members were entitled to the status of university professor.

By linking the development of the School of Political Sciences and the creation of the Business School to the Institute of Sociology, E. Solvay wished to emphasize the interplay noted between research and teaching in the fields of economics and sociology. The presence of the Faculties of Medecine also enhanced the Institute of Sociology's multidisciplinary character. By creating such close ties between personal foundations, university foundations and universities, he wished to participate in the creation of a coherent whole, whilst still retaining the management and orientation of certain research institutions. In the end, the Institute of Sociology would be transferred to the University but this was to be decided on by the Solvay family.

According to Armand Solvay, the Institute was in the first instance to be offered to the Society of Nations. It however declined the offer and the family then handed the Institute over to the ULB's Board of Governors. The family also provided a sum of 4 million francs, the interest on which was for the day-to-day management. Further conditions: the Institute was to remain a research institution and its founder's ideas would continue to be the object of certain studies. The ULB would supplement its budget up to a maximum amount of 25000 francs and would enter into agreement with the City Fathers on the continued and definitive tenure of the Parc Léopold buildings which, in accordance with the June 3, 1901 agreement, would be returned to the town's central authorities in 1926. This is the reason why the University and the central authorities agreed on a long-term lease in order to keep the Institute of Sociology in its original location.

The 4 million francs were invested at 5 % providing a yield of 200000 BF. Madame Solvay granted further sums of 65000 BF in 1926, 100000 BF in 1927 and the Solvay family provided 1 million in 1931 for the setting-up of a social survey department.

*

* *

This long chapter ought to be closed with a few words on the International Institutes of Physics and Chemistry, founded by Ernest Solvay, respectively on May 1, 1912 and May 1, 1913 for a period of thirty years. These were to be extended until 1949. Both institutions were set up with the aim of promoting research and progress in physical and chemical sciences. This was to be done notably through the holding of international scientific symposia; those would be held every three years similar to that which was held in Brussels in 1911 by the Belgian Physics Council. Ernest Solvay had brought together, from October 30 to November 3, the world's leading specialists. Among them: Marie Curie, Einstein, Rutherford, Max Planck, Poincaré, Langevin, Lorentz and the Duc de Broglie.

This meeting's dominant topic was quantum mechanics. Ernest Solvay had written a memoirs on the equivalence of energy and matter, a problem on which he had been working since 1858 with the hope of developing a satisfactory theory. It would appear that this subject was not debated by the scholars at

The Solvay Physics Council, Brussels 1927.
First row: Langmuir, Planck, Mme Curie, Lorentz, Einstein, Langevin, Guye, Wilson and Richardson.
Second row: Debye, Knudsen, W.L. Bragg, Kramers, Dirac, Compton, de Broglie, Born and Bohr.

the time of this meeting. Its author, however, was not dismayed and did not forgo his wish to set up, side by side with those of Sociology and Physiology, two International Institutes, one for Physics and the other for Chemistry. Matter, life and society were problems of the utmost interest to him. Although he was not a professional scientist, his work on the links between matter and energy led him to envisage the possibility of extracting energy from matter. Lorentz has said of him that he was Einstein's predecessor.

After his death, Madame Ernest Solvay and her children, greatly wishing to ensure the Institutes' future, signed an agree-

Third row: Picard, Henriot, Ehrenfest, Herzen, De Donder, Schrödinger, Verschaffelt, Pauli, Heisenberg, Fowler and Brillouin. Absent: W.H. Bragg, Deslandres and Van Aubel.

ment with the U.L.B., awarding it with their management. The University also received the Institutes' assets together with the necessary funds for the reconstitution in 1940, the expiry date, of a capital sum of one million francs which each Institution had been endowed with by its founder.

On October 17, 1963, on the occasion of the 50th Jubilee of their creation, they were given a new status which was intended to prolong and develop their activities.

When the University of Brussels was split into two independent institutions (one to be administered by the French-speaking community (U.L.B.) and the other by the Dutch-speaking community (K.U.L.)), the members of the administrative commission of the International Institutes of Physics and Chemistry's decided the moment was right to renew the structures in order to increase their independence and action without however prejudicing their influence and teaching. Subsequently, an association called «the International Institutes of Physics and Chemistry founded by Ernest Solvay» was launched for an unlimited duration in Brussels on July 22, 1970. Its purpose: the organization of Physics and Chemistry Committees, aiming to examine the important problems with which these two scientific fields are confronted and the invitation and participation of Belgian and foreign scientists in the University's scientific work (either for the U.L.B. or the K.U.L.).

The financial means put at the disposal of this center of excellence which still today pursues its activities are essentially provided by the two Universities' annual grants, revenues, profits and returns on its assets, voluntary grants from its members and other donations and bequests. In this way, the long tradition of organizing meetings and exchanges of ideas was maintained. These meetings which are still organized today and which still function according to their founder's ideas, are headed by Ilya Prigogine, Nobel Prize winner and chaired by Jacques Solvay.

Ernest Solvay wrote: «*You will never fully realize how greatly I wish to know and understand that which is, what we are, what the universe's true reality is and why it will go on for ever.*» Had all these ideas been abandoned, they would nevertheless have confirmed a natural concern for humanity. A great many have remained of topical interest; this can be seen in the flow of ideas and achievements they have brought forth.

An old view of the Torrelavega site, situated in northern Spain.

PART THREE

THE YEARS AFTER ERNEST SOLVAY'S DEATH

I. THE PERIOD BETWEEN THE 50TH AND 75TH JUBILEES

During the intervening 25 years, Solvay & Cie adapted its strategy to suit its new objective, i.e. expansion within continental Europe. Until then, it had been a mono-production multinational and its clients paid in advance for supplies. By basing its strategy on advanced technical organization, by accelerating the construction of new factories and promoting improvements which would lead to price decreases, the company was able to overcome the difficulties caused by the Great War and above all the Russian Revolution which had stripped it of three production units on Russian territory.

In addition, the company was confronted with two new elements: the law and American anti-monopolistic ideas; and the need to counter the German firm, I.G. Farben, in Great Britain

The Rosignano site in Italy, at the beginning of the century.

Tavaux (France), the Group's largest plant.

and the United States. Up to 1918, all the information gathered concerning the company's soda works was centralized in Brussels. This sodium carbonate cartel established the various zones of influence and gathered the information. For a while, the creation of Imperial Chemical Industries enabled this strategy to be maintained but due to circumstances, Solvay & Cie.'s new horizon was to be the European continent.

Immediately after the Armistice, the company bought up the

The original Povoa plant, Portugal.

soda works in Zurzach (Switzerland), in Monfalcone (Italy), in Povoa (Portugal), in Eisenach (West Germany) and the electrolysis plants in Pontemammolo (Italy), Hallein (Austria) and Aspropyrgos (Greece). All these various small units had been launched thanks to local initiative. Solvay modernized them and turned them into high-performance units, some of which still exist today.

In addition, he built a potash factory in Suria (Spain), soda works and electrolysis plants in Tavaux (France) and other electrolysis plants in the Netherlands, Spain and Portugal. The Borth salt mine was put into service and at the same time, the old factories were expanded to increase output and to promote the beginnings of diversification. In this respect, we would mention the Rosignano factory in Tuscany (Italy) where after many expansion stages, it has recently become the group's largest such unit, a whole new industrial complex having been added to the original unit. However, the most far-reaching decision taken during this period was without doubt the construction of a very large factory in Tavaux, in the Jura region of France. The French authorities were concerned that, in the event of hostilities, the safety of the Dombasle-sur-Meurthe site which was in close proximity to the German border could not be ensured. Some time later, in 1932, an electrolysis plant and soda works were built at the Tavaux site and was to be the last soda works built by Solvay. All future developments in this line of production would be carried out through the expansion of existing units.

As for chlorine, this continued to develop as Ernest Solvay had forecast. The company not only built electrolysis plants in Tavaux, as already mentioned, but also in Linne-Herten (the Netherlands), in Pontemammolo (Italy), in Torrelavega (Spain) and in Povoa (Portugal). This clearly demonstrates the company's policy

Linne-Herten in the Netherlands.

of setting up international production unit networks. In 1938, electrolysis production amounted to 30000 tons which was still insignificant compared with the quantities produced by the soda works. Nevertheless, the way had been paved for the future and the production programs were later to include chlorinated mineral by-products such as sodium and calcium hypochlorite, hydrochloric acid and chloride of lime. A little before the outbreak of World War II, Solvay entered the field of organic chemistry, producing trichlorethylene and perchlorethylene from chlorine. For the first time in the company's history, the sale of these products led it to address the marketing problems posed by these consumer goods. Solvay & Cie. has, since then, established increasingly close contacts with the end-consumer.

From then on, production ratios for chlorine and caustic soda would change and while the early producers of chlorine were busying themselves with finding outlets for their product, a very urgent problem needed solving. How to store the caustic soda which was an essential component in the production of chlorine?

II. THE PERIOD BETWEEN THE 75TH AND 100TH JUBILEES

The disappearance of lime-based caustic soda, the rising importance of chlorine, the reconversion of factories destroyed during the World War II and the loss of factories in eastern Europe were the most important events which marked this period. The company's 75th Jubilee had been celebrated in peace time before the outbreak of war. After Germany's capitulation, the company suffered a rude awakening: its production units had been bombed. In addition, about twenty of its premises (sites or factories), located behind the Iron Curtain and subsequently nationalized by the new regimes backed by the Russian army, were no longer under its control and had even become its direct competitors. Solvay thus lost its interests in eastern Germany. Among the factories which were lost was the Bernburg factory which was at that time the group's most important production unit. This was also to be the case for the Polish factories (where the future Pope, John-Paul II, was employed during the war before entering the priesthood), together with sites in Czechoslovakia, Romania and Yugoslavia. The communist regimes' successive coup d'états and nationalizations had, thus, stripped the Solvay Group of half its assets (in 1917 in Russia and in 1945 in Central Europe).

Yet the company's founders had instilled their successors with all their own energy and, despite the disruption caused by the war, the company continued its expansion with the construction in 1941 of its electrolysis plant in Rosignano, in 1942 of the Ferrare unit and in 1944 of the one in Zurzach. From 1946 to 1963, which was the company's centenary year, the Bayonne soda and salt works were built together with the electrolysis plants at Elclor (Brazil), for which plans had been drawn up during the war, and at Baba-Ali (Algeria). Polyvinylchloride (P.V.C.) plants at Jemeppe-sur-Sambre, Ferrare, Hallein, Tavaux, Elclor and Rheinberg, together with chloromethanes factories at Ferrare, Jemeppe-sur-Sambre and Tavaux were also erected. Polyethylene complexes were set up at Rosignano and Elclor; hydrogen peroxide perborate units were launched at Jemeppe, Tavaux and

Rosignano together with an allytic plant and plastics factory at Tavaux. Last but not least, a cat-cracking unit was built at Rosignano.

Since the company was forced to rebuild its factories, it took the opportunity of modernizing and expanding its production tools. Such progress had been made so quickly that the group's severely curtailed production outstripped its 1938 tonnage (i.e. when the company still controlled all its assets). Solvay was about to start out on new productions and to expand its scope. The company had already decided in 1941 on establishing its presence in Brazil, under the leadership of the future company chairman, René Boël. This was to be the beginning of very important business and production activities in this rapidly developing nation.

The implications of the company's centenary year require some consideration. Ernest Solvay had died in his sleep on May 26, 1922. His death was not the end of the company's development but the 1950's were to be difficult times for the company's managers due to the fact that production was based on one product, alkali. The senior managers were engineers and not business men and were exclusively of European origin. Had these trends not been reversed, the company's expansion would have halted.

Plastics, plastics processing and health, the Group's new business sectors.

The post-war years saw the development of plastics. P.V.C. (polyvinylchloride) which had been analyzed in the company's laboratories, seemed to be promising. Its main characteristic was that it used up chlorine manufactured by the group as well as acetylene which was obtained from calcium carbide via the coal by-products industry. It was thus a non-petroleum based plastic and it is therefore quite understandable that the chemical companies gave it all their attention. Through its 25% holding in Imperial Chemical Industries (I.C.I.), Solvay obtained the technical know-how and built production units, on its own or in conjunction with I.C.I, first at Jemeppe-sur-Sambre and then at Hallein, Ferrare, Tavaux, Torrelavega, Rheinberg and Elclor. Over the years, the group was to become the leading P.V.C. producer. Once again, this is based on its policy of products integration together with the development of an international network of factories.

A product's financial returns can result in repercussions felt upstream. P.V.C.'s rapid development, in association with other chlorinated products, thus led to the worldwide expansion of chlorine production. The Solvay Group was very active in this development. Its massive involvement in this field compelled it

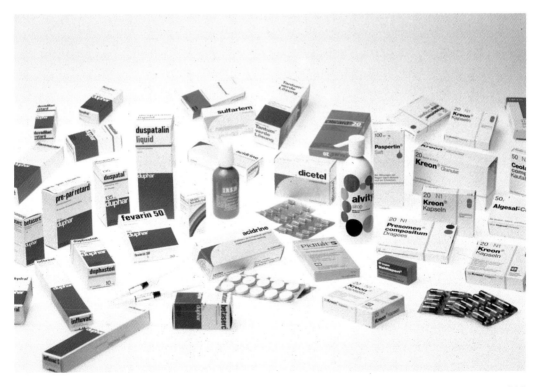

to take the leading position. Besides consolidating existing units, other electrolysis plants were built at Elclor, Rosignano, Ferrare, Zurzach and even Baba-Ali, which was sold back to Algeria in 1962 at the time of this country's independence.

In addition to P.V.C., Solvay entered into the production of chloromethanes (at Ferrare, Jemeppe and Tavaux) and allytic products such as glycerine (at Tavaux).

The group's general development of chlorine led to increased production of caustic soda of which Solvay was the world's No.1 producer. The causticizing process was in slow but definite decline, disappearing totally, however, only after 1963.

The pace of production was maintained due the increasing uses of carbonate, notably in glass production and above all in the construction trade, motor industry and bottle manufacture. It did a great deal better than just compensate for the decline of the causticizing process.

However, chlorine was not the only reason. Electrolysis of brine also produced a by-product: hydrogen. It had few applications and was only put to good use as a fuel. This led Solvay to study the production, via the quinon process which uses *The Rheinberg plant in Germany.* hydrogen, of hydrogen peroxide, sold in diluted form by chemists. Production units were set up at the same time at Jemeppe, Tavaux, Hönningen and Rosignano. The fact that these plants were erected simultaneously is proof of the confidence that the research results and the group's expansion policy inspired. Solvay had become a manufacturer of chlorine- and hydrogen peroxide-based oxidizing agents. The production of persalt, for use in washing powders, was annexed to the hydrogen peroxide units and soon peroxide output developed sufficiently at Solvay for it to become one of the group's five main productions.

This post-war expansion, after a period of severe losses, was also to continue in other areas.

The war had limited the company's activities in Germany because of the confiscation of the units located in East Germany. In West Germany, Solvay only exploited the soda works at Rheinberg and the Borth mine which had been opened in the inter-war years. Both sites were to be expanded.

In the 1950's, it became necessary to increase the group's presence in West Germany, thanks to a favorable economic climate, via a majority interest in the company Kali-Chemie. The control of this subsidiary had the double advantage of con- *Kali-Chemie, a Group subsidiary in* solidating Solvay's products on the market and interesting the *West Germany.*

114

company in new fields. Indeed, Kali-Chemie was developing products such as barium and fluor derivatives which were similar to Solvay's products, not only from the technical but also from the commercial point of view. The originality of this acquisition was that it incorporated a pharmaceutical division into the existing group. This was to be the beginning of a greater involvement in this field.

Yet, before Solvay became as totally involved as it is at present, the company mastered another important turning point for its future: the processing of plastics and notably its own P.V.C. Until then, Solvay products were bulk products for very widely varying industrial applications, not directly involving the end-consumer. Solvay's entry into the P.V.C. processing industry was to have several positive effects: the company was to become involved in consumer goods, to deal with marketing problems and to ensure outlets for its synthetic resins. Through its own effort to create and expand, the group started producing corrugated plastic sheeting and bottles. Subsequently, due to the acquisition of the Maréchal company in France and to the fact that this company had developed a very diversified production program, including vinyl wallpapers, Solvay became involved in the production of rolled sheeting and coated textiles. All this gives some indication of the company's development and gradual diversification process.

Solvay's central management was fully aware of the dangers involved in the production of a single resin, P.V.C. It, therefore, decided to develop its product range and the first new product was Ixan, a «barrier» resin, produced at Tavaux. However, the company's main effort was in the field of polyethylene, first at Rosignano and then at Elclor.
The Brazilian subsidiary was to produce the necessary ethylene from sugar cane alcohol.

In 1963, Solvay celebrated its centenary. During the preceding 25 years, the group had sustained its unceasing expansion. This not only concerned its products but also its sites which had been completely transformed since the precarious situation of 1938. A new company structure based on divisional organization for plastics and the older products (salt, alkali, chlorine) had replaced the old mono-production multinational group. This on-going transformation was to be maintained.

*Elclor, a Group
subsidiary in Brazil.*

III. THE PERIOD BETWEEN THE 100TH AND 125TH JUBILEES

The first tests at the gas plant in Saint-Josse-ten-Noode, the difficult early years at the Couillet factory, the first patent in 1861 and the discovery that the process had already been developed and the resulting rivalry... are all long passed events. The history of the Solvay company is that of courageous and visionary people and minds intent on the future. They foresaw that during the 1950's, there would be an extraordinary industrial challenge to be met: the transformation of the company's production itself and investment in new fields.

At that time, Solvay was still a limited partnership and was one of the world's largest companies to have retained this structure. It was not a very well-known company, preferring to be discrete by remaining a family concern, based on advanced production decentralization together with centralization of technical data and overall strategy. General management and the day-to-day running of the company were based on collegial decisions due to the partnership's joint responsibility. The company's original statutes did not allow it to raise the necessary funds to meet the challenge of the post-war period and to implement the industrial development program drafted by Ernest-John Solvay, his brother-in-law, René Boël and later Jacques Solvay.

It was decided that the best arrangement for the company would be to become a Joint-Stock Company which took place in 1967 on the basis of an initial capital of BF 10 billion (later to be increased to 12 and subsequently 32 billion BF). Over roughly 20 years, the net dividend per fully-subscribed share increased from 120 to 335 BF. The Group's daily management had to change radically. The accounts which had previously remained secret for more than one century had to be made public which of course meant that the company as a whole came under general scrutiny.

In addition, an American consultant advised the company directors to appoint experienced and capable outsiders to their midst. He devised a matrix structure which is still in use 25 years later. It is in this way that some divisions have set up «product

...phar in the
Netherlands, a
Group subsidiary
with activities in the
human health
sector.

commissions» where experienced and competent personnel (technical and commercial staff, as well as researchers) come together from all levels within the Group to discuss problems and to make suggestions. This form of organization works well and explains Solvay's enduring success in the face of a very difficult commercial climate due to the fact that the company no longer has its former production monopoly. To sum up, the new legal status integrated these organizational factors and the business strategy on which the company's old foundations had been established. Furthermore, Solvay reaffirmed its determination to be the leader or among the leading producers of its range of manufactured goods, while maintaining its multinational organization.

The setting-up of an active commercial sales force, the development of the Brussels research laboratory and the consolidation of the national managements called for an in-depth reorganization which was carried out in 1968. This led to the management of a greatly diversified group which would undergo further in-depth developments. A framework was introduced, based on three distinct, yet closely linked, departments. Multidisciplinary structures were set up providing the different departments with the necessary expertise:

— policy and strategy departments, situated in Brussels, defining the company's outlook and development, in other words its future;

— logistical services, providing technical, financial and human resources assistance;

— implementation services, i.e. local administrations and their production units, dealing with production and sales.

In addition, the industrial production tool was adapted to enable the various branches to develop at their own speed according to the economic situation which is the overriding factor in each company's day-to-day management.

The massive production of chlorine led to surpluses of caustic soda which were processed into sodium carbonate in specially adapted soda works. Electrolysis plants were set up next to the Dombasle and Rheinberg soda works and two others were built on the open sites of Antwerp and Martorell, in Spain where vinyl chloride and P.V.C. production was also launched.

In 1970, Solvay joined up with Laporte Chemical Industries Ltd of London under a joint venture called Interox which grouped the interests of the two companies in the field of hydrogen peroxide and its derivatives. Through this joint venture, Solvay entered the British Commonwealth. Interox would later expand worldwide and is at present the group's largest network of subsidiaries. The activities in the organic peroxide field provided by the English partner were subsequently developed and expanded. At the same time, Solvay bought up a 25% share in Laporte.

The P.V.C. units continued to be developed but Martorell, near Barcelona, was to be this sector's only new production site after the company's centenary year. On the other hand, it became apparent that P.V.C.'s future could no longer be ensured by the monomer obtained from calcium carbide. A very large-scale and expensive reconversion operation had to be organized: from now on, the monomer plants would use petroleum ethylene. Units based on this new process were built at Jemeppe, Tavaux, Rheinberg, Martorell and Elclor. Solvay was in a better position to manage the P.V.C. production on its own after I.C.I., had divested its remaining 25% interest in the jointly-owned subsidiaries between 1982 and 1985, due to the 1981 plastics crisis, excepting the Hispavic subsidiary in Spain.

In order to avoid the dangers arising out of mono-production of plastics, Solvay resolutely turned towards the development of another resin, high-density polyethylene. Even before its centenary year, the group had become involved in its production under licence from another company. However, the research laboratory at Neder-over-Hembeek was only really satisfied once it had developed its own high-performance technique which was immediately applied at the Sarralbe, Rosignano and Elclor plants and was later also partially introduced at Deer Park, Texas.

At this point, it ought to be said that Solvay had been looking for the right moment to set up units in the United States. The right occasion was to occur in 1974 when it took over the Celanese Corporation's, Texas, polyethylene activities. This initial acquisition was to become a very important and highly diversified production center located at Deer Park, east of Houston. Its subsidiary, Interox, produced not only high-density polyethylene there but also polypropylene and hydrogen peroxide.

Solvay was not only concerned with completing its range of resins but had also decided to promote its own polypropylene production based on an in-house technique developed by its Neder-over-Hembeek research team.

Furthermore, several research projects concerning special resins, also known as technical polymers, were launched. These polymers had increasing importance in Solvay's production range.

As for the processing of plastics, this sector was very rapidly developed through an extensive in-house effort and through acquisitions in various areas such as calendering, coating, bottles and flasks, pipes, gasoline tanks, etc. The securing of the German company, Alkor, together with the Dutch firm Draka Polva, were to be the two main acquisitions in this field. Processing at Solvay diversified not only regarding the items produced but also from the point of view of the resins employed.

However, one of the two most unexpected turns of events to occur during recent times was to be the company's involvement in the pharmaceutical and veterinary industries. Whereas Solvay had been mostly involved in inorganic chemistry in the 19th and 20th centuries, becoming a major player after 1950 in the worldwide development of plastics, it was in the 1970's that it embarked on a totally new venture: the Life sciences, i.e. biochemistry giving rise to biotechnologies which in turn open up vast new opportunities in the health care sector. To this end,

Reid-Rowell in the United States (human health).

Salsbury, an American subsidiary with activities in the veterinary sector.

biochemists were trained to enable the company to respond to ever-increasing demand.

The purchase of the American company Salsbury in Charles City, Iowa, immediately gave Solvay a good international position in the field of animal vaccines. The German subsidiary Kali-Chemie increased its involvement in the pharmaceutical field by initiating an acquisitions' policy, notably in France (Latema, Sarbach) and in Germany (Giulini). This policy was also to be applied in various countries, among them Spain. The new group approach was continued with the acquisition in 1980 of Duphar, the Dutch group Philips' pharmaceutical subsidiary which already had a multinational organizational structure and an important research establishment at Weesp, near Amsterdam. The two subsidiaries, Kali-Chemie and Duphar, were very largely complementary, not only from the point of view of products but also from their geographical location regarding production and commercialization. This led to the development of very positive and profitable synergies, favorably reinforced by the acquisition in 1986 of Reid-Rowell, an American company, and Unione Chimica Medicamenti of Italy.

The second new development was the launching in 1970 of the group's activities in Asia, via the Interox Group, which bought up an interest in Nippon Peroxide, Japan and National Peroxyde, India.

This initial step was to be followed soon after by the setting-up of Solvay-Marubeni Chemicals in 1975, also in Japan and in 1981, of Kali-Duphar which was the foundation stone of Nippon Solvay, established in 1986.

Another decisive measure was the creation of a management center in Singapore, together with the setting-up of associate offices in various Asian countries. This was to be the starting point for a series of sites in South Korea, Hong Kong, India and Thailand, some of which will certainly be successfully developed. Asia is currently experiencing the world's highest growth rate. The Solvay Group has always been present in those regions where the best conditions for expansion are present.

The 1973 world energy crisis certainly had an incidence on Solvay just like the rest of the chemical industry. However, right from the start of its history, the company had had to tackle major energy saving problems in order to ensure its soda production technique's leading position. As a result, the company has evolved its own way of doing things which the recent world crisis has only further emphasized. The technical departments put their minds to the task at hand and thanks to wise investments, they were

The Group's expansion in Asia: Solvay representatives in Singapore.

Solvay in the United States: the Deer Park plant in Texas.

very rapidly able to draw up efficient and wide-ranging savings programs.

These 125 years have witnessed the long and steady development giving rise to the cohesive group described in the following chapter.

THE PRESENT SITUATION

I. A GENERAL SURVEY

The year 1988 was both Ernest Solvay's 150th birthday and the 125th Jubilee of the company named after him and his brother. In 1944, their company was present in thirteen countries. Today, it is present in thirty two, of which eighteen are in Europe, providing employment for about 45000 people. Solvay is Belgium's second largest industrial group after Petrofina and ranks respectively 10th and 17th among the European and international chemical companies. However, concerning a wide range of its products, it ranks among the world's main producers: No.1 producer of sodium, barium and strontium carbonates, high-density polyethylene, peroxide products and vitamine D, No.2 producer of salt and No. 4 for P.V.C. and chlorine production. Solvay has built or acquired some 300 premises around the world.
The different world markets are thus supplied by local production units which explains the fact that exports remain modest, compared with overall turnover. This consequently makes Solvay less susceptible — compared with other European groups — to monetary fluctuations. These companies benefit from major decentralization in the fields of production and sales, but the Group's industrial policy is defined by the Central Administration located in Brussels.

The Solvay company must nevertheless be considered as an industrial company with some specifically financial units. The founders were industrialists and their program was industrial. They wished to be producers themselves or to produce in conjunction with a top-level partner but only if this was really necessary and as rarely as possible. Solvay has never become a holding group.

Due to its endeavors not to digress from its original purpose, the Group has concentrated its efforts on a limited number of activities where it has great technological and commercial expertise. At Solvay, personal initiative and enterprise and the wish to progress and develop are actively encouraged. This attitude has remained a company tradition and not only explains the delegation of powers and the decentralization but also the emphasis laid on professional training and individual job satisfaction.

One essential concept pervaded the whole organization ever since its creation, based on three principles: technical mastery, supply of raw materials, the will to reach a key position in each

Festivities for Solvay & Cie's 125th Jubilee: a Gala Concert was held on October 11, 1988 at the Théâtre de la Monnaie, Brussels, in the presence of T.R.H. The King and Queen of Belgium.

sector. This three-tiered concept led to soda's prime position and, even before 1900, caustic soda and chlorine were also to be successful thanks to the arrival of the electrolysis process. The road towards production of a wide range of organic and inorganic derivatives had been opened up and this was pursued with great strides.

In 1949, Solvay launched the production of P.V.C. and a short while later, other plastics such as high-density polyethylene (HD-PE) and polypropylene (PP) were also introduced. At about the same time, the chemistry of oxydizing agents was developed, opening the way for exploration of peroxides and their derivatives.

Having once become the world's leading producer of P.V.C., it is only natural that it was also interested in the field of plastics processing, i.e. calendering, coating, extrusion, blowing, thermoforming, etc. And then, to prove the company's youthfulness, other sectors were investigated where no one was expecting Solvay's presence, such as pharmaceutics, veterinary products, special polymers and biochemistry.

The inorganic products of Solvay's debut, i.e. sodium carbonate, caustic soda, salts, calcium products and chlorine to which barium and strontium carbonates, fluorated products and industrial and motor car catalyzers, grouped under the term alkalis, must be added, now represent 30.7% of the Group's turnover. The peroxide products account for 7.4%, plastics for almost a third, more precisely 31.8%, processing 18.1%, pharmaceutics which include medicinal and veterinary products, crop protection products and biological products, totalling 12% of turnover.

This brief list suffices to show the importance that Research & Development is given at Solvay. The founders gave it their undivided attention and their descendants and successors would do likewise.

In 1893, Dr. Wilsing, a chemist at the Bernburg factory in Germany studied and developed the first diaphragm electrolysis cell.

Barium titanate, a ceramic used in electronics and produced via a technique developed by the Central Laboratories, Brussels (enlarged 20000 times).

However, it was not until slightly before World War II that a small research laboratory was set up in the Central Administration's cellar at Ixelles. It was soon to become the Central Laboratory, moving to its own building in the same street, just opposite the company's headquarters.

In 1940 it employed several dozen people and by 1950 this figure had greatly increased, reaching 150 and continuing to

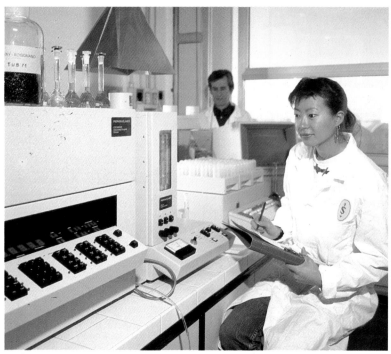

The Solvay Group's research effort is worldwide; exchanges of knowledge and the many different cultural backgrounds are contributing factors.

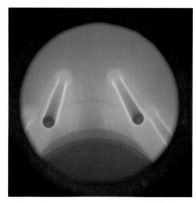

Kali-Chemie is studying inorganic fluorides for use in sophisticated applications such as fiber-optics for halogen glass.

Surface-modification of a polymer sheet due to plasma polymerization (opposite).

Solvay's IXEF® polyarylamide rocker cover has been chosen by the motor industry, due to its very great dimensional stability (opposite).

New polymerization methods are being developed in our laboratories (at right).

rise, forcing the Administration of the day to choose a new site near Brussels. Those were in short the beginnings of the Research Center which is now located at Neder-over-Hembeek and which at present has a staff of 1300 people.

At the same time and in order to translate the scientific research into industrial and production successes, pilot units were set up at the Group's main factories: Tavaux, Jemeppe, Dombasle, Rosignano,...

If one were to include the Group's subsidiaries' research centers such as Kali-Chemie in Hanover (West Germany), Duphar in Weesp (The Netherlands) or Salsbury in Minneapolis (U.S.A.), then the research teams can be considered as totalling some 3300 scientists.

Research & Development are resolutely turned towards the future and today's major investment effort will bear the fruit of things to come.

Each of the group's five main areas of activity, i.e. alkalis, peroxides, plastics, processing and health, is responsible for the R & D strategy in those areas with which it is in direct association. Yet, an overall strategy aims to diversify the Group's range of products and business activities and to develop new technologies. This strategy is managed by the Central Research Administration which also deals with general business coordination of the Group's thirty or so research centers.

Solvay recruits scientists from all over Europe, from the United States and elsewhere, not only to satisfy its local requirements but above all to acquire scientific expertise and know-how from all horizons and different educational backgrounds. About a dozen nationalities are represented within its research teams and eight different languages are spoken.

One in every fifteen members of staff is recruited to work directly in research; one scientist in every four is a university graduate. However, it is said that Solvay employs 45000 scientists, thanks to the very great team spirit which unites all its members of staff whether researcher, production or marketing personnel.

A great many research contracts very clearly demonstrate Solvay's high regard for collaboration with the universities; basic research is considered as essential to the process of innovation.

Today, everyone recognizes the very important role played by research. At Solvay, research has many different but not contradictory purposes, ranging from finding solutions to clients' problems, improvements to the production process and the products' quality, the development of new drugs and technologically-advanced materials and finally to protection of the environment.

Each of the five business sectors reaps the benefits from the research results. Yet, parallel to the development of new inorganic raw materials for use in micro-electronics or in fiber-optics, the alkali department is still engaged in trying to understand fully the soda works invented by Ernest Solvay, endeavoring to improve both yields and the quality of the produced carbonates.

Computer technology has of course become a powerful new tool able to simulate industrial techniques, to design installations, monitor its functioning and ensure safety.

All these aspects of research, linked to chemical engineering, vital to the engineers who are in charge of the units' construction and production, have been grouped under the management of the Technology Administration.

This same computer technology, coupled with the most sophisticated methods of physico-chemical analysis, has also led to great progress in the understanding of molecular structures and their links to microscopic properties.

Is it not every chemist's dream to discover the properties of a new substance or of a new drug?

Since the creation of the Group, Solvay has been closely involved in organic chemistry, i.e. initially sodium carbonate and then caustic soda, leading on to those essential raw materials for use in the glass and metal industries. This involvement dates from shortly after World War II, starting with the production of P.V.C.

One should therefore not be surprised if the research not only focuses, to a large extent, on the development of new properties for its existing thermo-plastics production (polyvinylchloride, polyethylene and polypropylene) but also on the expansion of its production range to include higher quality products which modern industry demands, whether this concerns the motor, electronics, aerospace or just simply the construction or packaging industries.

A molecule's intrinsic properties do not, however, alone dictate the finished product's expected performances. Research into new substances, polymers and others, has made it necessary to set up experimental workshops to test these new materials. These workshops finalize the company's three-point strategy concerning development and technology of chemical substances: properties — production technique — performance.

*The Solvay Group
has always paid
special attention to
its personnel's on-
going professional
training.*

*Safety of the
installations requires
an efficient and
up-to-date
infrastructure: the
Company's own
fire-brigades are
given special
training at most of
the Group's plants
(at left).*

*Twenty-four
Company doctors
from ten different
countries meet at
10th Solvay Medical
Meeting held in
Amsterdam in April
1988 (at right).*

International seminars are organized, uniting members of staff from around the world and from the company's various departments, in order to develop a common work ethic and high quality management throughout the Group.

Structure — properties: this also is a challenge for all the research scientists working in the health sector and which today represent nearly half the Group's personnel.

The conversion of ideas into new drugs implies a very long and complex process, full of uncertainty and financial risks. Hundreds of new molecules have to be examined before finding one which shows sufficient promise to justify further research. The new drug will thus have been submitted, for over ten years, to very severe internal and external selection trials before becoming a prescription drug. It is thus vital to focus research on several promising areas: the Solvay Group has chosen to concentrate on the cardiovascular system, the central nervous system, on gastroenterology and immunology, four areas where clinical needs for new drugs are very great and where its researchers know that they can provide new and better drugs.

Important financial means are also provided for the veterinary sector where biological products are the main research objective. Solvay only very rarely boasts of its know-how. It is not particularly well known that the first commercial genetically-engineered vaccine (the ECOBAC® vaccine for diarrhoea in piglets) was developed in collaboration with university research.

Ernest Solvay believed that Science would provide the means for humanity's progress. This same belief still inspires the Group's research scientists some 125 years later. Their talent and enthusiasm play a vital role in the improvement of production techniques, in the search for solutions to clients' needs for products of increased performance, patient relief and environmental protection. For these men, research is the means by which to improve their fellow-men's quality of life.

The founders' efforts continued along the same lines and according to the same ideas regarding material and social concern. The Group's social and staff policies remain one of the management's main areas of consideration. The personnel department employs about 850 people throughout the world of which 80 manage social policies, primarily at Central Administration and also at the national and subsidiary levels. The remainder deal with human resources management at local level.

They assist top management in implementing the major directives regarding employment and integration of young people, together with training, mobility, promotion, assessment and detection of each member's talents, information and participation. They also engage in the search and selection of personnel, human resources management of active and retired members of staff, contacts with staff representatives and the outside world, problems concerning staff redeployment and matters of health, without mentioning their contribution to staff motivation and morale.

Exchanges of executives from the different continents often take place at Solvay, enabling each of the sites concerned to benefit to a maximum from experience gathered elsewhere, to train men of the broadest vision possible in order to be able to deal with the many problems which may arise in their specific fields and to appoint those most suitable to positions of high-responsibility and multidisciplinary managerial duties.

It is for this reason that expatriate executives are to be seen at Central Administration or in factory or department management teams. Others are sent abroad as specialists to contribute to the application of technologies in which they have a sound knowledge and good experience acquired at home.

Yet others, the youngest, are given assistant managerial functions where they are trained to deal with all the varying aspects and problems concerning a large group whose business activities cover many countries. This organization is complex since local adaptability is linked to an overall common strategy decided on by the Group's senior management. The scope and rapidity of modern means of communication greatly assist its application.

Since on the international level, talented executives are followed so that they may reach their full potential, transfers to other parts of the world are frequent events and decided on by mutual agreement. Although material and personal problems may arise due to these transfers, the human resources management team strives to minimize these difficulties.

Each of the Solvay sites develops an annual personnel training scheme taking local needs, based on the staff's levels of qualification and the development of new technologies, into consideration. At one given site, one may decide to provide training for young members of staff with no particular qualifications or with good theoretical knowledge. Elsewhere, in-house training programs of several months' duration give the best workers access to higher qualifications.

This organizational structure shows the special attention that is given to the instructor's role for the many discussion groups on progress, expression, job security and on quality control which have been set up at various production sites.

No one will be surprised to learn of the importance which

Insoluble sulphur, CRYSTEX®, is one of the compounds used in high-tech tyres (at left).

Salt used for clearing snow is Solvay's contribution to road safety (above).

Salt beads, produced at the French plant in Bayonne, are used to cure ham.

A catalyzer used in cars equipped with a catalytic exhaust and designed to filter exhaust fumes.

Strontium carbon and barium carbonate are used in the production of special high-grade glass.

Sulphur hexafluoride, KALTRON® 14 and KALTRON 22 are high-purity plasma etching gases used in the production of integrated circuits.

In the background: brine-stocking facility in Povoa (Portugal).

is given to in-house circulation of information. The company's managers are well aware of its vital necessity and geographical expansion. Each member of staff is kept informed of internal and external developments via the exposés provided by the different administrations, the in-house news bulletins and magazines. However, nothing can replace one-on-one verbal communication. The art of speaking is, however, not given to everyone. In this respect, each member of staff is given the chance to improve his public speaking abilities to a maximum. News and other information are essentially provided by the company's in-house bulletins and magazines.

This rapid survey of the Solvay's present state will be rounded off by a brief examination of the Group's policy concerning job safety and health hazards. Safety is an attitude of mind which has to be sustained at all levels and at all times. Accident and risk prevention programs together with heightened awareness training and safety drills have been worked out and put into effect. The constantly updated safety measures are systematically audited. These studies show that the safety recommendations must be appropriate and investments must be made, based on present technology, to improve general safety levels which results

The Borth salt mine, in West Germany, is the world's largest rock-salt deposit. Two views of salt-mining taken in 1934.

The glass industry is a large consumer of sodium carbonate with uses in the motor, packaging and construction industries.

Oy Finnish Peroxides AB, the Interox Group's Finnish subsidiary (opposite).

Peroxydos do Brasil in Curitiba (Parana State) (below).

Salt mining and excavation in Borth of the enormous underground chambers.

Interox Chemical's hydrogen peroxide plant in Banksmeadow (Australia) (at left).

Hydrogen peroxide is used notably for bleaching paper pulp and textiles.

Water treatment, the Interox Group's contribution to a cleaner environment.

in very low accident rates.

Central Administration and the local administrations attach such importance to their personnel's welfare and to the worksites' cleanliness that their industrial medical departments meet periodically to benefit from each other's experience and know-how.

*Interox Chemicals
Ltd. hydrogen
peroxide production
unit in Warrington
(Great Britain)
(following pages).*

II. THE PRODUCTS

Reference was made in the introduction to the world's biggest salt mine, located in Borth, West Germany. Ernest Solvay used to say, «Where there is salt, we must act». The mine's reserves are so great that even at today's rate of extraction of more or less 2.5 million tons per year, extraction can continue for decades. A machine, 800 meters underground resembling a prehistoric monster and called the Marietta, excavates a 50 km network of galleries in the salt mine. Enormous trucks which have been reassembled underground, transport the extracted salt to conveyor belts from where it is brought to the surface and loaded onto goods cars or mixed with water and transferred in brine solution to the soda works, thanks to a pipeline which connects, amongst others, Borth to Jemeppe-sur-Sambre.

Calcium is the other raw material used by the Solvay soda works. Sodium carbonate is manufactured, on the one hand, from limestone and carbonic acid, from the lime furnaces, and on the other hand, from salt extracted from the brine solution. The product is then dried by industrial dryers, turning it into a white powder.

The soda works also produce other by-products of which the main one is calcium chloride, used to salt the roads in winter. Only infinitesimal amounts of these enormous heaps of extracted salt and manufactured sodium chloride are used in the housewife's kitchen. The salt at Solvay is mainly used in the soda works and in the electrolysis process, manufacturing other products to meet industry's many demands. Thanks to electricity, electrolysis can be used to produce chlorine, caustic soda and hydrogen. The manufactured chlorine takes two different directions on exiting from the electrolysis plant: firstly, it is used as a solvent and, secondly, in the production of vinyl chloride which is the most important basic ingredient in plastics.

The biggest consumer of soda products is industry itself, the main one being the glass industry. Two hundred to 250 grams are necessary to manufacture 1 kg of glass. One hundred kgs of caustic soda are used to produce 1 ton of soap, 200 kgs are necessary to produce 1 ton of aluminum and 600 kgs are required to manufacture 1 ton of cellulose. Sodium carbonate is used in the metal industry to desulphurize cast iron and is also used in

The new NYREF® resins complete the Group's barrier-polymer range offered to its clients.

159

The P.V.C. resin BENVIC® HPT's low permeability to oxygen and UV-barrier make it particularly suitable for use in the packing industry, especially for oils and carbonated or flat mineral waters (at left).

The CLARENE® barrier-resins are particulary suitable thermoplastics for use in the packaging of foodstuffs and other products.

Solvay's high-density polyethylene is used in the production of 3-layer, coextruded flasks for use in bottling UHT milk.

the textile industry, in the production of linen, wool and cotton, and in the treatment of cellulose. It is not widely known that soda is also used in petroleum refineries, in the pharmaceutical and food industries, as well as by wine-growers (5 kg of sodium bicarbonate for every 10 hectolitres). It really is a universally used product.

The name Solvay makes one immediately think of soda but this is not the company's only product. In the 1950's, its managers came to realize that the company either had to adapt or disappear. At the time of Yalta and the subsequent division of Europe, Solvay lost its potassium, salt, lignite and coal mines together with seven ammonia-based soda works, three electrolysis plants and two cement works. All these units were located in East Germany, Poland, Hungary, Czechoslovakia, Romania and Yugoslavia. The expropriations and the confiscation of its Russian factories, thirty years earlier, meant that Solvay had been stripped of virtually half its assets.

To survive, the company had to replace these losses but how? The Group's head office made the following statement: «We must strive for perfect technical mastery in those areas where we have decided to expand our operations». After soda, salt, calcium products and chlorine, the Group chose to launch production of peroxides, essential in bleaching, since they optimize the hydrogen which is a by-product of the electrolysis process. Subsequently, the company also entered production of plastics, starting with P.V.C. which requires vast quantities of chlorine and then the plastics processing sector. Finally, Solvay also became involved in the health care and veterinary sectors, through its acquisitions and subsequent subsidiaries. Each of the large group of products merits close examination.

ALKALIS

Alkali production capacity, as such, is over 6 million tons per year and this activity still represents more than 20% of overall turnover. The soda products are used as basic ingredients in industry (glass, metallurgy, textile and paper) and can be found in a great many every-day uses. Two main types of sodium carbonate are offered: light and dense sodas, for use in the glass, soap and metal industries and more generally in basic chemistry.

Caustic soda which can be supplied in either 50% or 72% solution or in solid form (beads, flakes or sticks) is used in the textile industry, in pulp, detergents, aluminum and throughout the chemical industry, without forgetting its many household uses.

Who has never taken some bicarbonate of soda or at least had some in the family medicine chest? It is also added to animal foodstuffs and is used in special form in fire extinguishers.

Substances with very scientific names such as sodium tripolyphosphate, sodium silicates, metasilicates and sesqui-carbonates are used in the manufacture of detergents.

As for salt production, it reaches 12 million tons annually.

Precipitated calcium carbonate is used as bulk for plastics, compounds, fine papers, paints, tooth paste, rubber, etc.

Sodium hypochlorite as well as concentrated sodium hypochlorite are used as a disinfectant for waste waters (private or public). Chlorinated lime is used as a general disinfectant and finally, rock-salt, vacuum salt and solar salt are also used in the chemical industry, as well as in other types of industries, in foodstuffs, for water-softening and to de-ice the roads in winter.

Mention has already been made of calcium chloride which is used as an additive for concrete, as an industrial refrigeration agent, as a dust protection agent and household dehumidifier. It is also used in the manufacture of phase shift materials used in the accumulation of low temperature thermal energy.

As a reminder, as early as 1898, Ernest Solvay exploited the world's first electrolysis process of sodium (salt) chloride on a mercury cathode in order to produce caustic soda, hydrogen and chlorine in great quantities. Chlorine was only considered as a by-product until 1949, at which time it really took off thanks to the Group's involvement in the production of vinyl chloride and thus its indirect association with the production of P.V.C. Its annual production has now reached 1.8 million tons. Produced in parallel to caustic soda, it also plays a part in the production of dichlorethane, vinyl chloride monomer and P.V.C., as well as in the pulp and paper industry. Moreover, it is used as a disinfectant and in the treatment of waste waters and inorganic and organic chemistry.

Ferric chloride, either in solution or in solid form, is used as a flocculation agent in water-cleaning operations and the treatment of waste waters as well as an etching agent for electronic circuits.

As for sodium chlorate, it is used for the bleaching of pulp as well as a weed killer and chemical oxidizing agent.

The company produces a great number of organic

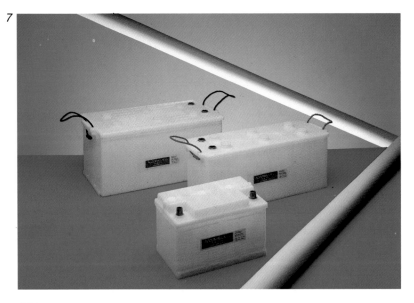

1. High-pressure
gases, waste and
drainage waters are
transported in
Solvay's
high-density
polyethylene pipes.

2. P.V.C. recycling:
the outer layer of
the coextruded pipe
is made from
recycled P.V.C.
bottles.

3. Extrusion head at
the Draka plant
(The Netherlands)
used in the
production of tubes
for medical
purposes.

4. Solvay provides the packaging industry with polypropylene copolymer films.

5. A roll of P.V.C. film.

6. P.V.C. resins are used in various medical applications.

7. Battery cases for the motor industry are made of polypropylene block copolymers.

The IXAN® coextruded barrier polymers guarantee the freshness and maintain the aroma of quick-dried coffee.

chlorinated derivatives which total 350000 tons annually. They have very complicated names that only the specialist can remember. Some of them, however, are household names, for example: chloroform. This is further proof of their wide-ranging uses.

It is sufficient to know that they are either primary or secondary substances for gasoline and rubber additives. They are also used in aerosols and paint-strippers, in dry cleaning, in grease removers for metals, in solvents for the electronics industry, in weed killers and in the pharmaceutical and food industries.

Solvay is also a producer of barium and strontium derivatives which have wide-ranging uses in the chemical industry, in steel and glass works, in paints and above all in the electrical and electronics industries where they are used to produce television and computer screens.

Finally, in the field of environmental protection, a great variety of catalyzers have been developed and are produced by the Group for use in the motor industry. Yet others are used in the petrochemical industry or as an air and gas drying agent.

PEROXIDE PRODUCTS AND THEIR DERIVATIVES

In 1970, Solvay and a British firm, Laporte Industries, joined forces in the peroxide products industry and set up the Interox Group.

This Group includes 19 companies, together with 8 associated companies and carries out worldwide production on 20 different sites which it supplies virtually on its own. What is hydrogen peroxide used for? Mainly for the bleaching of pulp and textiles but also in the production of polyesters and polymers, in environmental protection, in the treatment of metals, in chemical synthesis, etc. Hydrogen peroxide is one of the 200 peroxide products and derivatives commercialized by the Solvay Group. Further to the production of hydrogen peroxide, the company also manufactures sodium perborate for use in detergents and cosmetics, organic and persulfate peroxides, primarily used in the polymer industry, peracetic acid for disinfecting equipment used in the food industry and potassium permonosulfate added to cleaning agents, disinfectants, in the treatment of waste waters, etc.

Solvay's and Laporte Industries' expertise in the field of research is obviously of great advantage to Interox. This joint venture disposes of significant funds and is engaged in a considerable

166

research effort to improve its products and their applications, as well as to develop new products and production techniques.

PLASTICS

Plastic products are such every-day items that we hardly notice them at all anymore. Plastic is used in the production and manufacture of such varied items as window frames, pressure hoses for gas pipelines, office equipment and accessories, bottles and containers for foodstuffs, shopping bags and holdalls. Plastic is truly a versatile material.

The term «plastic» covers different materials such as polyvinylchloride (P.V.C.), high-density polyethylene (HD-PE), polypropylene and «barrier» resins which are used in the packaging industry.

Solvay has been involved in the plastics industry since 1949 and ranks as one of the foremost producers of P.V.C., with a production capacity of nearly 1 million tons a year. Solvay is also the world's leading producer of high-density polyethylene, with an annual production of 900000 tons. The different production units are located in Europe, Brazil and the United States.

We shall enumerate some of these extremely common finished products. There is a very good chance that some will have been produced by Solvay: electrical cables, imitation leather, anti-corrosion compounds for cars, battery cases, blinds and shutters, bottles for general packaging purposes (detergents and motor oils), plastic bottles for milk, gasoline tanks, industrial-size containers for the construction industry, the red plastic cones used by the police and road workers and also toys, crates and stoppers for all types of bottles and plastic flasks, handling containers, plastic strips for the textile industry, etc., etc.

Solvay produces polypropylene both in Europe and the United States which has a thousand and one uses in the motor and also the packaging industries (the plastic film around cigarette boxes). Moreover, in order to improve still further productivity and the quality of its resins, the Group is developing new high-performance catalyzers for its polypropylene production.

The «barrier» resins are very widely used in packaging, especially for foodstuffs. Why are they known as «barrier» resins? This is due to their excellent sealing qualities concerning steam, dry aromas and gases, especially oxygen. In the first instance, they are used in textile coating, composite paper materials and

The new FORD
THUNDERBIRD's
plastic gasoline
tank, produced by
Hedwin Corp., one
of the Group's
American sub-
sidiaries.

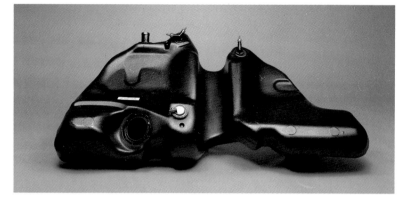

The alveolated and
thermoformed
NESPACK® plastic
fruit and vegetable
baskets are much
appreciated by
supermarkets for
the packaging and
presentation of
foodstuffs
(opposite).

Griffine-Maréchal,
one of the Group's
French subsidiaries,
produces highly
creative, top-class
vinyl-coated textiles
(at right).

Plastic tubing pro-
duced in Spain at
Saenger S.A.'s
Tube Division.

ONDEX®,
a bi-dimensional
corrugated plastic,
has especially good
resistance and light
transmittance
characteristics
which are of
particular interest in
the manufacture of
greenhouses
(at left).

low-density polypropylene, sheet aluminum and plastic film, for paints, varnishes and printer's ink, extrusion and co-extrusion of films or sheets; in the second instance, they are used in the production of anti-oxidizing packaging for such products as, among others: fruit juices, fats, milk produce, pre-cooked meals, sauces and condiments.

PROCESSING

Solvay became interested in the processing of plastic materials during the 1960's. Its involvement in this area has been most successful since becoming one of the leading plastics processors. The initial objective of this diversification was to acquire a better understanding of the problems encountered in plastics processing in order to provide clients with an improved service.

This production represents about one fifth of the Group's overall turnover and covers the following sectors:

— industry, with two products: firstly, rolled and extruded sheeting or film (300 million square meters annually of P.V.C. sheeting and polypropylene) which are used in paper mills, small leather goods, food and pharmaceutical packaging, as well as wood veneering and metal plating, silk-screen printing and electrical insulation; secondly, imitation leather for use in the cloth trade and the shoe and furniture industries;

— in the motor industry: for upholstery and interior finish, bumpers, gasoline tanks and other special containers;

— packaging, using plastic bottles for mineral waters, oil, vinegar, wine, thermoplastic packaging, small plastic containers for fruit and vegetables, small drums and hollow structures;

— the construction industry, concerning both construction itself and decoration. For the first-mentioned sector: plastic pipes and connecting pipes, corrugated P.V.C. sheeting, wall protections, special mortars, outside wall insulation, water-proof sheeting for roofs, swimming pools and for use in civil engineering, wood protection agents, wood- and metal fire-proofing agents... For the second-mentioned sector: wall furnishings, wall papers and vinyl wall papers (over 25 million rolls produced annually), fabrics and foam rubbers, tablecloth fabric and curtain material. Could one ever have imagined that, only shortly after the end of World War II, there would be such a profusion of synthetic materials not only in factories and offices but also in the street and in every home?

Increased consumption has meant that they have become wholly indispensable.

Had Solvay not reached its present level of mastery in the field of wood protection, the world's largest wooden building, the Buddhist Temple at Nara in Japan, would have vanished for ever. The building was saved through restoration work using Xylamon, a Solvay product. The company's processing activity thus not only handles plastics but also touches on chemicals.

HEALTH CARE

The Solvay Group has recently and rapidly developed its interest in the Life sciences: biochemistry, biology, biotechnology.

Historically speaking, this is its third scientific line of development: firstly, inorganic and then organic chemistry and finally, the Life sciences.

Through its subsidiaries it has quite naturally come to produce insecticides and also acaricides and weed killers. It commercializes enzymes and peptides and is the world's No.1 vitamin D producer, basing production on an original process which uses cholesterol from sheep's fat as its basic raw material.

Solvay is at present among the top 50 pharmaceutical companies in the world. This position stems from the acquisition of subsidiaries which were well-established in this industrial sector. The two companies, Duphar and Kali-Chemie, represent Solvay on nearly all West European markets as well as in India, in the Philippines, in Indonesia and in Japan. Reid-Rowell, its American subsidiary, acts as its representative in the United States.

The following drugs, available at the chemist are produced by Solvay:

Duvadilan® and Neo-gilurytmal®: for cardiovascular diseases;

Baldrian® and Floxyfral® for treatment in medical conditions related to the central nervous system;

Duspatalin®, Duphalac®, Pankreon®, Creon®, Acidrin®, Dicetel® and Paspertine® for gastro-intestinal treatment;

Duphaston® and Prepar® (known as Yutopar® in the U.S.A.) for use in obstetrics and gynaecology;

Algesal® and Liman® for rheumatism;

Imudon®, IRS 19® in immunology;

Influvac®, the anti-flu vaccine;

and various other hormone specialty drugs.

P.V.C.
AIKORPLAN®
membrane used in
China to ensure
isolation of the
reactor core.

Solvay ranks as the
12th most important
producer of
veterinary products,
taking the lead in
vaccines for poultry,
pigs, cats, dogs and
horses.

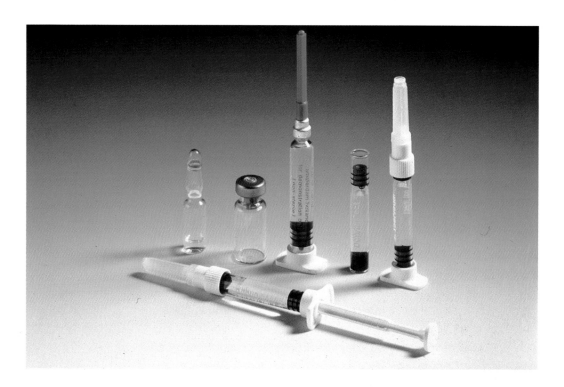

The DUPHARJECT® pre-filler seringe is much appreciated on all Solvay's markets.

FLUVOXAMINE is a particularly efficient antidepressant for use in the treatment of disorders of the central nervous system.

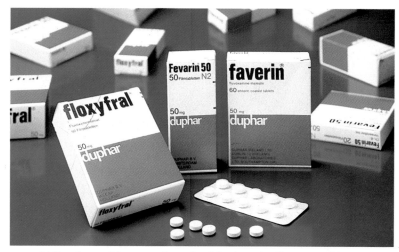

At the time of its entry into the biochemical sector which shows great promise, the company has also become involved in the field of animal health. Solvay ranks as the world's 15th most important company in this sector.

The integration of such firms as Salsbury Laboratories Inc., Fromm Laboratories Inc., Duphar Nutrition Inc., Solvay Veterinary Inc., located respectively in Iowa, Wisconsin, Illinois and New Jersey, United States and Duphar B.V., in Weesp (The Netherlands) into the Solvay Group has meant that human, technological and commercial resources have been grouped together, leading to the setting-up of a special unit to deal with development of research activities and new markets.

Solvay's veterinary department is specialized in vaccines for poultry, dogs, cats, horses and pigs as well as various other veterinary products, food additives and vitamins.

Such a vast international network which includes 15 national organizations and marketing activities in more than 24 countries has enabled the Solvay Group to establish a quite extraordinary power base, not only due to its geographical diversity but also to the quality of its products and research effort.

Thanks to this, Solvay has demonstrated its will to remain at the forefront of biotechnological progress in research and production, whilst expanding its commercial strength and cultivating its human resources. The company, founded in the second half of the 19th century by two unknown individuals, on the banks of a river, without any other ambition than being one of the most industrious companies of a newly-born nation, has now come of age and can look to the future with confidence.

III. THE FUTURE

One hundred and twenty-five years have already past. Since then...

Solvay is now present on the five continents. No doubt, the company is not so widely present in Australia, Africa and Asia as it is in Europe or America but it is nevertheless part of the industrial landscape. Some political events, without which the Group would no doubt have been successful, have obliged it to abandon certain endeavors. Success will be achieved elsewhere since it is Solvay's purpose to be present there where there is a suitable site, together with ready raw materials and production possibilities.

After more than twelve decades, the Group shows no signs of flagging. The general public's confidence in the company is reflected in the increased value of its shares which are quoted on the Brussels, Antwerp, Amsterdam, Basle, Berlin (free quotation), Düsseldorf, Frankfurt-am-Main, Geneva, Paris and Zurich Stock Exchanges. The Group is in flourishing financial health. The annual business reports are there to prove it.

Today, Solvay is present throughout the world, being located in 32 countries, that is to say 290 towns, locations or sites. Just another small effort and the 300 mark will have been reached. This event will surely not be long in coming.

Will one remember in 2063 that 200 years earlier the factory, launched at Couillet in 1865, produced 200 kgs of sodium carbonate compared with the 1200 tons which had been forecast? Had Ernest Solvay, helped by his family and investors and assisted by his brother, not tackled the various individual problems as and when they arose and had he not solved them by finding original solutions and innovations, this book would not have been written and the Solvay name would have remained obscure and little known.

Following on its founders and on history, the Solvay Group is today the proud beneficiary of five very successful sectors, four of which are closely interconnected. The fifth which is the health care sector is a natural development of the company's overall interests. The high added value precision work based on detailed research is not considered as an independent and separate offshoot but as a fully-integrated department, working in symbiosis with the company's other sectors. These have also developed

Special foam spray-on conditioning of the antirheumatic ALGESAL® makes for easy drug administration. View of the susbsidiary Kali-Duphar's production unit in Spain.

Water treatment plant at Duphar, a Group subsidiary in Weesp, The Netherlands (photo: KLM AEROCARTO-Schiphol).

parallel high-technology activities, involving state-of-the-art specialization, as is the case for special polymers.

Products which have come to fruition, such as soda and P.V.C., provide abundant cash-flow which is used to finance newer products which have not yet fully matured. Thus assisted during their developmental stage, they are given maximum financial support in order to succeed, to consolidate their position and in turn provide support for the next generation of products. The various development graphs thus show productions at all different stages.

Throughout the 125 years of existence and already at its founders' instigation, this graph's starting point was and still is continually modified and improved. The overall structure forms a stable and healthy organization.

What does the future hold for its wide-ranging production activities? What will their respective places be within the Group in the next ten or twenty years' time? Let us look closely at the five sectors in order to be able to answer these questions.

The *alkalis* which represent 32.1% of the Group's turnover, are a range of products in which Solvay is generally the world's leading producer, or at least among the top producers. This was the case, at the outset, for sodium carbonate which represented at that time 100% of the Group's production but which now only represents about 10%. It is not that this production has decreased. Quite to the contrary, it has never ceased to increase but other productions have gradually grown in importance and size.

All these products are manufactured in enormous quantities and have very high margins. Solvay is also engaged in long-term investments to modernize its plants. At present, electronics reign supreme, be it P.C.'s in all the engineers' offices or in the production unit itself, for application in the automatic regulation of the distance between the electrodes in the brine solution, or even the complete automation of the production process.

This sector's outlook is that good results and cash-flow will be maintained but that growth will not be as high as in the other sectors and will thus show a drop in its share of turnover.

The *peroxides* total 8.2% of sales, and as has been mentioned, are produced in association with the British group, Laporte. The Interox joint venture is a world leader in its field. Peroxides are also produced in extremely large quantities and provide high profit margins. They also have the special quality of not being vulnerable to market fluctuations, their levels of production being quite untouched by economic crises or periods of prosperity.

Interox's market position is very strong since it is involved in sophisticated production, entailing serious risks for the uninitiated. The setting-up costs concerning investment, research and development of the production process, are extremely high for a new-comer to this type of production.

The future will, in all probability, see good results and this sector will represent an increasing share in the Group's production activities.

Plastics which now account for 27.7% of Solvay's turnover, are no longer the mass-produced industrial productions they used to be. The Group has thus developed a wide range of different P.V.C.'s, polyethylenes and polypropylenes. These different qualities have been developed in response to increasing high-performance requirements made by the products' users, such as, for example, the electronics and motor industries and the various medical applications.

Solvay is increasingly engaged in the development and production of very special high-quality plastics with particular specifications, integrating high added value and invulnerable to economic crises.

As for this sector's fourth activity, i.e. special polymers, they are by definition high-technology products complying with the extremely high-temperature, high-pressure and high-corrosion resistance levels required.

At Solvay, downstream integration is applied in the production of plastics. This is to say that the Group uses its own productions which it then processes, transforming them into finished products. This integration shields the company, to some extent, from economic instability, enabling it to finalize its technology for resin production which looked very promising at the time of its launch.

The expectations for this sector are that the technical polymers will gain increasing ground and that this sector will expand faster than the rest of the Group. Results are also expected to continue improving.

Processing which represents 19.8% of total turnover will also benefit from the above-mentioned integration. A great number of the raw materials used in this sector are provided by the parent-company.

This business activity has gained an important position on the special products' market, for example polyethylene gasoline tanks for the motor industry and makes increasing use of state-of-the-art technology. Solvay's level of competence in this field gives it the leading edge over its direct competitors.

Furthermore, Solvay's management is engaged in an investment policy to consolidate its positions in those areas in which the Group is technologically and commercially superior.

The *health care* sector which accounts for 12.2% of turnover is a relatively new area of business for Solvay.

In human medicine, the Group has concentrated on four

The Alkor plant (West Germany) has invested DM 12 million in a gas-emission treatment plant (solvent and plasticizer vapors).

areas of therapeutics (gastro-intestinal and cardiovascular therapy, neurology and immunology). Solvay has already achieved a very strong position in Europe, in the United States and in Japan. The critical limit has been reached in the four specialty areas; they now need to be consolidated and developed. The recent acquisition of the American firm, Reid-Rowell, showing major synergies with the European subsidiaries, enables Solvay to plan for the introduction of its European products which will lead to an important place on the American market. The research effort will thus be optimized, thanks to the size of that market, twice that of Europe. The setting-up in 1989 of the Solvay-Meiji joint venture will form the basis of the Group's presence in Japan, the world's third-largest market. This joint venture has also established a sales' network in the rest of Asia which will without doubt expand successfully.

As for animal health, Solvay's very strong position in the field of animal vaccines (poultry, pigs, horses, dogs and cats) will lead it to become the world's No.1 producer of such products. Here too, new and specifically-designed products are being developed.

The company's overall strategy has always been to concentrate on high-profit productions in which it leads the world, technically and commercially.

With this in mind, Solvay has chosen to limit itself to five activities, each one's development being based either on the internal growth of existing means or on the acquisition of outside activities, providing the necessary funds.

The company intends to maximize high-profit and high added value productions, such as the health care and technical polymer sectors, whilst at the same time, increasing its geographical diversification, especially in the United States and in Asia.

To reach these objectives, the company has tried to achieve the necessary levels of investment in order to guarantee the Group's high productivity, together with an equally high level of research which will give the in-house-developed technologies world-leadership.

The company's increasing degree of prosperity provides it with the necessary means for achieving these objectives. Despite investments which have, for the past five years, increased from 8.3 billion to 23.7 billion BF annually and a research effort which has increased from 6.5 billion to 10.8 billion BF, the company's financial situation has been consolidated to such an extent that income has equalled and now even outstripped financial debts. This is truly a unique situation in industry. Solvay's management is thus better equipped to face economic uncertainties and can seize interesting opportunities to strengthen the group further in its chosen areas of development.

To conclude, one may state that wisdom and vision have been the company's guiding light throughout its existence, determining its present financial stability and ensuring a bright and promising future for Ernest Solvay's monumental achievement.

Following pages: Ernest Solvay not only founded a major company but also an extended family. His descendants gathered on October 15th, 1988 at the «Ernest Solvay Mansion» to celebrate the company's 125th Jubilee. The company's three most recent Chairmen, Count Boël, Mr. Jacques Solvay and Baron Daniel Janssen can be seen seated in the first row.

REFERENCES

Louis Bertrand: Ernest Solvay, réformateur social (Brussels) 1918

Jacques Bolle: 1863 — 1963 Solvay L'invention — L'homme - L'entreprise industrielle (Brussels 1963)

Louis D'Or, Anne-Marie Wirtz-Cordier: Ernest Solvay (Brussels 1980)

Institut Solvay: Notes concerning the Foundation of the Institute of Physiology, Parc Léopold,Brussels, (Brussels 1910)

Jacques de Launay: La dynastie des Solvay (Paris-March, November 1, 8, 15 and 22, (1985)

R.T.B.F. Charleroi: Film on Ernest Solvay

L. Viré: la «Cité scientifique» du Parc Léopold

The author wishes to express his gratitude to the various members of Solvay & Cie.'s staff for their kind collaboration in the preparation and correction of the present manuscript.

INDEX

WORKS BY MAXIME RAPAILLE

Published by Didier Hatier Editions

Le Chant des Wallons, Vol I, fiction (1988)
Le Chant des Wallons, Vol II, to be published

Printed by other publishers

Les Guibert, fiction (1951)
La première mort, fiction (1954)
Le jeu impossible, fiction (1956)
Le fils de la femme adultère, fiction (1958)
Maris... et autres hommes, short stories (1961)
Une semaine perdue, fiction (1966)
Les temps heureux que nous vivons, play (1971), including:
      Il n'y a plus de liberté - Les vainqueurs - Voici venue la dernière heure
Les neiges du cœur, fiction (1972)
La patrouille assassinée, narrative (1974)
La montée au Golgotha, fiction (1974)
À distance égale, essay (1975)
D'autres hommes... d'autres femmes, short stories (1976)
Les colères vaines I, chronicles (1977)
Corinne ou un amour indien, fiction (1980)
Six morts au carrefour, fiction (1984)
      prix Tchantchès 1985.
Histoire d'un roman, essay (1985)
Le chancelier d'un été, fiction (1985)
À Brochant, peut-être?..., fiction (1988)
Mourir en paix, fiction (1988)

Play

Des millions en fumée, 1960.
Agression à main armée, 1965.
Escale à l'aéroport national, 1977.

Radio-play

Agression à main armée, 1967.

Printed in Belgium